Mary Shelley's
FRANKENSTEIN

Bloom's
NOTES

Edited and with an Introduction by
HAROLD BLOOM

© 1996 by Chelsea House Publishers, a division of Main Line Book Co.

Introduction © 1996 by Harold Bloom

Printed and bound in the United States of America.

First Printing
1 3 5 7 9 8 6 4 2

ISBN: 0-7910-3689-8

Chelsea House Publishers
1974 Sproul Road, Suite 400
P.O. Box 914
Broomall, PA 19008-0914

Contents

User's Guide

This volume is designed to present biographical, critical, and bibliographical information on Mary Shelley and *Frankenstein.* Following Harold Bloom's introduction, there appears a detailed biography of the author, discussing the major events in her life and her important literary works. Then follows a thematic and structural analysis of the work, in which significant themes, patterns, and motifs are traced. An annotated list of characters supplies brief information on the chief characters in the work.

A selection of critical extracts, derived from previously published material by leading critics, then follows. The extracts consist of statements by the author on her work, early reviews of the work, and later evaluations down to the present day. The items are arranged chronologically by date of first publication. A bibliography of Shelley's writings (including a complete listing of all books she wrote, cowrote, edited, and translated in her lifetime, and important posthumous publications), a list of additional books and articles on her and on *Frankenstein,* and an index of themes and ideas conclude the volume.

Harold Bloom is Sterling Professor of the Humanities at Yale University and Henry W. and Albert A. Berg Professor of English at the New York University Graduate School. He is the author of twenty books and the editor of more than thirty anthologies of literature and literary criticism.

Professor Bloom's works include *Shelley's Mythmaking* (1959), *The Visionary Company* (1961), *Blake's Apocalypse* (1963), *Yeats* (1970), *A Map of Misreading* (1975), *Kabbalah and Criticism* (1975), and *Agon: Towards a Theory of Revisionism* (1982). *The Anxiety of Influence* (1973) sets forth Professor Bloom's provocative theory of the literary relationships between the great writers and their predecessors. His most recent books are *The American Religion* (1992) and *The Western Canon* (1994).

Professor Bloom earned his Ph.D. from Yale University in 1955 and has served on the Yale faculty since then. He is a 1985 MacArthur Foundation Award recipient and served as the Charles Eliot Norton Professor of Poetry at Harvard University in 1987–88. He is currently the editor of the Chelsea House series Major Literary Characters and Modern Critical Views, and other Chelsea House series in literary criticism.

Introduction

HAROLD BLOOM

Frankenstein; or, The Modern Prometheus is the full title of Mary Wollstonecraft Godwin Shelley's inaugural science fiction novel, which she began before she was nineteen and finished less than a year later. Mary Shelley's full name is as important in understanding *Frankenstein* as is the book's full title. The novel intends us to see its protagonist, Dr. Victor Frankenstein, as the modern Prometheus, stealing creative fire from heaven in order to make a creature, a New Adam, whom most of us now call "the monster," because we have seen so many motion picture versions of *Frankenstein*. Despite his crimes, the creature is as much angel as monster, and we do best by following the book in calling him "the daemon." This ill-starred daemon is, in certain respects, a critique of all three illustrious figures who meet in Mary Shelley's full name: her mother, the radical feminist Mary Wollstonecraft; her father, the radical philosopher William Godwin; and her husband, the revolutionary lyrical poet Percy Bysshe Shelley. These three great idealists all had envisioned a new humanity in a newly structured society, and all had hoped that human nature could be redesigned, so as to eliminate exploitation, timidity, remorse, and conventional morality. Though Mary Shelley, to some extent, shared in these aspirations, her book nevertheless is a powerful, implicit critique of the Romantic Prometheanism of her husband and the radical rationalism of her parents.

The center of *Frankenstein* is the bitter relationship between Victor Frankenstein and his daemon, best expressed by the daemon when he cries out to the scientist: "Remember that I am thy creature; I ought to be thy Adam, but I am rather the fallen angel, whom thou drivest from joy for no misdeed." This alludes to the novel's epigraph, Adam's lament to God in John Milton's epic, *Paradise Lost:*

> Did I request thee, Maker, from my clay
> To mould me man? Did I solicit thee
> From darkness to promote me?

One way to measure the vast distance between Mary Shelley's daemon and the movies' monster is to try to imagine anyone of the film monsters educating himself by reading Milton's *Paradise Lost.* Mary Shelley's formidable daemon does exactly that, and receives a superb education in consequence. Unlike Victor Frankenstein, who is a literalist lacking in imagination, the daemon has the sensibility of an authentic poet. Critics tend to agree that Frankenstein and the daemon are the two halves of the same being, divided against itself. This gives an ironic sanction to the universal popular "error," by which the name of Frankenstein has come to mean the poor monster rather than its irresponsible creator. When we realize that, in the book, the creature is far more sympathetic than its maker, then we approach the heart of Mary Shelley's critique of the two men she loved best, her father and her husband, and of the mother whom she never knew, since Mary Wollstonecraft died in giving birth to the author of *Frankenstein.*

Though *Paradise Lost* is so crucial an influence upon *Frankenstein,* the novel's genre more closely resembles Jacobean revenge tragedy. What Frankenstein and his daemon ultimately desire is revenge upon one another. Each might say, with one of the revengers in John Webster's *The White Devil:* "I limned this night-piece, and it was my best." The book's final night-piece is its best, as Frankenstein and his daemon seek their final confrontation in an Arctic frozen sea. And yet the entire book is a night-piece, since it represents the torments of a civil war in the Promethean psyche, fought out between Frankenstein and his daemon. The daemon is superior to his maker both in spirit and in feeling, and so we come both to love him and to fear him. We do not have any particular affect towards the scientist who has both botched his work (the daemon is hideous in appearance) and failed to take responsibility for his creature. It is one of Mary Shelley's many fine ironies that the daemon mourns his dead maker, hardly an emotion that Victor Frankenstein would have experienced had he succeeded in slaying his creation.

The relevance, aesthetic and moral, of Mary Shelley's novel only augments as we enter more deeply into an era that already has brought us "virtual reality" and seems likely to confront us with cyborgs. Victor Frankenstein, though he possesses generous impulses, is nothing less than a moral idiot in regard to the "monster" he has created. Even at the end, he cannot understand his own failure of moral imagination, and he dies still misapprehending the nature of his guilt. He is thus at once a great Hermetic scientist, an astonishing genius at breaking through human limitations, and a pragmatic monster, the true monster of the novel. His trespass is beyond forgiveness, because he is incapable of seeing that he is both a father, and a god, who has failed to love his marred creation. The novel's greatest strength seems to me its ironic contrast between the deepening of self-consciousness in the poor daemon and the narrowing of self-awareness in Victor Frankenstein. There are no victors in Mary Shelley's plangent novel: Frankenstein and the daemon both end in defeat. Yet the daemon has a tragic splendor, while Frankenstein is at most a figure of pathos. Our current purveyors of "third wave" future shock, and their political allies, ought to ponder the deeper meanings of Mary Shelley's Promethean parable. ✤

Biography of
Mary Shelley

Mary Wollstonecraft Godwin was born in London on August 30, 1797, the only daughter of the philosopher William Godwin and the feminist writer Mary Wollstonecraft, author of *A Vindication of the Rights of Woman* (1792). Her mother died ten days after giving birth to her, and in 1801 Godwin took a second wife, Mary Jane Clairmont, whom Mary passionately disliked. Mary received no formal education, since her stepmother favored her own daughter, Jane. However, her father frequently held literary gatherings with the most distinguished writers of the period, including William Hazlitt, Samuel Taylor Coleridge, and Charles Lamb, and Mary developed literary leanings from these encounters. In 1806 Coleridge read his supernatural poem, *The Rime of the Ancient Mariner,* at such a gathering; Mary and her stepsister, Jane, defied their curfew and heard Coleridge's recital while hiding behind a couch. Her first published work was a poem printed in a magazine in 1808.

In 1812 Godwin sent Mary to live in Dundee, where she remained, except for brief visits, until 1814. During one of these visits, at the end of 1812, Mary met Percy Bysshe Shelley and his wife, Harriet. After meeting a second time in 1814, Percy and Mary fell in love and left England together, accompanied by Jane Clairmont (who now called herself Claire). They traveled through France, Switzerland, Italy, Germany, and Holland. Both Mary's father and her stepfather strongly disapproved of the liaison, and Mrs. Godwin went to France to persuade Mary to come home; but she refused. During this trip Shelley sought to practice his notions of free love, encouraging Mary to have an affair with a lawyer, Thomas Jefferson Hogg, while he himself had an affair with Claire.

In 1815, after Mary, Percy, and Claire had returned to England, Mary gave birth to a daughter, who died less than two weeks later; of their four children only one, Percy (b. 1819), survived infancy. Later in the year they returned to Switzerland, where they set up a house on Lake Geneva near a villa owned by Lord Byron. Harriet Shelley, shattered by her husband's infidelity, committed suicide in November 1816. Shelley and Mary Godwin were married on December 30, 1816.

In 1817 Mary Shelley anonymously published the *History of a Six Weeks' Tour*, cowritten with Percy. The following year her most famous work—and one of the most famous novels of the nineteenth century—was published: *Frankenstein; or, The Modern Prometheus*. It was the product of a contest among Mary Shelley, Percy Shelley, Lord Byron, and John William Polidori as to who could write the most frightening tale; Mary's was the only one brought to a conclusion, although Polidori produced the able short story "The Vampyre." *Frankenstein* was published anonymously, as were several of Mary's later books, and was thought to be the work of a man until the revised edition appeared in 1831.

Shortly after the publication of *Frankenstein*, Mary and Percy left for Italy. Still disturbed by her father's continued hostility to her marriage, she wrote a novella, *Matilda*, about father-daughter incest; it was published only posthumously. On July 8, 1822, Percy Shelley was drowned in the Bay of Spezzia during a heavy squall.

Because Mary did not wish to surrender her only remaining child, Percy, to Shelley's father, Sir Timothy, the latter refused to give any financial support, and it became necessary for Mary to support herself by writing. Over the next fifteen years she produced five novels: *Valperga* (1823), a romance about medieval Italy; *The Last Man* (1826), a powerful apocalyptic work about the last man on earth (a figure modeled clearly upon Percy Shelley); *The Fortunes of Perkin Warbeck* (1830), an historical novel in the manner of Sir Walter Scott; *Lodore* (1835), a heavily autobiographical melodrama; and *Falkner* (1837), another autobiographical work whose protagonist is based upon Percy Shelley's friend Edward John Trelawny. After Percy's death, Mary considered proposals of marriage from several individuals, including the actor John Howard Payne, the American writer Washington Irving, and the French novelist Prosper Mérimée, but her devotion to Percy's memory remained steadfast and she refused all these overtures.

During the period 1828–38 Mary also wrote many stories for the *Keepsake,* and in the early 1830s she produced five volumes of biographical sketches of "eminent literary and scientific men" for *Lardner's Cabinet Cyclopedia* (1835–38). A two-volume travel book, *Rambles in Germany and Italy in 1840, 1842, and 1843* (1844), was the last work published in her lifetime. Mary Shelley edited and published her husband's *Poetical Works* (4 vols., 1839) and his *Essays, Letters from Abroad, Translations and Fragments* (2 vols., 1840). She died in London on February 1, 1851. ❖

Thematic and Structural Analysis

In the 1831 "Author's Introduction" to *Frankenstein*—thirteen years after its first publication—Mary Shelley explains how, at the age of nineteen, she conceived the frightful story of Victor Frankenstein and his creation. Being born to two distinguished writers (Mary Wollstonecraft and William Godwin) led her to write at a very early age, and as a pastime she wrote fanciful stories for herself and her childhood companion. She recalls "peopling the hours with creations far more interesting" than herself and the ordinary world around her. Later, her husband, the poet Percy Bysshe Shelley, urged her to follow in her parents' "glory" by writing professionally. In 1816 she and her husband spent the summer in Geneva, Switzerland, with the poet Lord Byron, where they shared a book of German ghost stories to pass the hours indoors during what proved to be a particularly rainy season. It was Byron who proposed that each of the friends write a ghost story to share with the others. Mary Shelley's was the only story to be completed.

In addition to documenting the autobiographical circumstances that led to writing *Frankenstein,* Mary Shelley's introduction also reveals the dramatic and thematic content of the novel. Shelley remembers listening to many philosophical discussions between Lord Byron and her husband while trying to think of a story that would "speak to the mysterious fears of our nature and awaken thrilling horror." One discussion focused on "the principle of life," the experiments of Dr. Darwin (Erasmus Darwin, the grandfather of evolutionist Charles Darwin), and the possibility of bringing a corpse back to life. It was this discussion that sparked the idea for Shelley's story, "for supremely frightful would be the effect of any human endeavor to mock the stupendous mechanism of the Creator. . . ." Shelley's stay in Geneva also provided the location for her story. Following the literary conventions of Romanticism, the setting of her tale is more than a geographical backdrop. The powerful natural landscape of Switzerland, and nature itself, play a major role in the novel and exert a tremendous influence on the main characters. The novel also adheres to Romantic conventions in that it narrates experiences charged with powerful emotions, many of which the characters experience alone.

Frankenstein begins with a series of four letters from Robert Walton to his sister, Mrs. Saville, who lives in England. In **letter one** we learn that Walton is embarking upon a scientific expedition to the North Pole and that reading of heroic sea voyages as a child has inspired him to "accomplish a great purpose" by discovering the secrets in "a part of the world never before visited." Walton ends the letter by admitting he may die in his attempts to satisfy his "ardent curiosity." Though brief, this letter introduces the novel's major Faustian theme of the dangerous consequences of thirsting for knowledge, particularly scientific knowledge pertaining to the secrets of nature.

Letter two introduces the novel's second major theme: loneliness and the human need for companionship. In updating his sister on the progress of his journey, Walton laments that his greatest difficulty is that he has no friend, no one near him to sympathize with or support him. He experiences this absence as "a most severe evil." Walton is closer to beginning his voyage; he has enlisted courageous sailors for his ship, yet none can satisfy his need for a companion or confidant and he realizes he surely will find no friend on the "wide ocean." He again tells his sister how passionately he awaits his expedition to "unexplored regions, to 'the land of snow and ice.' " In this explicit reference to Coleridge's famous poem *The Rime of the Ancient Mariner* Walton alludes to another character who sins against nature. The reference also acknowledges the influence of the Romantic poets on Mary Shelley's novel.

Four months elapse before the **third letter,** which merely states that Walton is well under way on his journey. His ship is already very far north and his crew members bravely observe the icebergs that float dangerously close. Walton speaks with certainty of the discoveries that must await him: "[T]he very stars" will witness his "triumph," Walton proclaims, for "what can stop the determined heart of man?" In these words Walton reiterates his yearning to claim the mysteries of nature, foreshadowing the passion of the young Frankenstein to discover the mystery of life.

The real story of *Frankenstein* begins in the **fourth letter** because it is here that we first meet Victor Frankenstein and see a fleeting glimpse of the man he created. A few weeks after the previous letter to his sister, Walton and his crew find themselves surrounded by ice. Though they suppose they are many hundreds of miles from land, they observe in the distance the form of an unnaturally large man on a sled being pulled by dogs. They watch this giant man with telescopes until he and his sled disappear in the ice fields. The next morning Captain Walton comes on deck to see his crew talking to a different man floating on an ice block alongside the ship. This man also has a sled, but only one dog remains alive. Though the man is clearly exhausted and sure to die if left behind in the icy water, he refuses to come aboard the ship until he learns that Walton and his crew are headed further north. The man boards the ship and promptly collapses from hunger and extreme fatigue. Walton takes him to his cabin, where the traveler recuperates. During the ensuing days of rest and nourishment, the man exhibits an extraordinary sensitivity and intelligence—and a profound despair—all of which deeply move Walton. It seems that, perhaps, Walton may have found a friend at sea after all.

Shortly thereafter the stranger reveals how he had come to such a dangerous situation on the ice so far from other living creatures: he was pursuing someone who fled from him. The stranger is told of the giant man seen in the distance the day before he was rescued. This news greatly excites him and soon he is well enough to keep continual watch on deck for the man he seeks. In the meantime, Captain Walton becomes more impressed with the stranger's demeanor and grows more attached to him. He describes him in angelic and brotherly terms: the man is a "divine wanderer," "a celestial spirit that has a halo around him." But he is more like a fallen angel or a broken spirit because even his gentleness and great intelligence cannot help him bear whatever immense grief consumes him. When Walton confides his yearnings for knowledge and discovery, and his willingness to sacrifice everything in this pursuit, the stranger despairs and decides to share his own tale of misfortune in the hope of saving Walton from a similar fate. From this point on in the novel the stranger, Victor Frankenstein, narrates.

In **chapters one and two** Victor Frankenstein tells of his birth and childhood. He was the eldest son born to a distinguished family in Geneva. When he was five his mother adopted Elizabeth Lavenza, a girl of noble parents left in the care of a peasant family in Milan and abandoned. Victor remembers the happiness of his childhood with Elizabeth, whom he called "cousin." Elizabeth was calmer than he and enjoyed poetry; while Victor thirsted for knowledge and desired to uncover "the secrets of heaven and earth." Victor also remembers his dearest friend, Henry Clerval, who was more interested in society and history than "natural philosophy." In addition to foreshadowing the dangers of wanting to know the sacred workings of nature, these chapters also advance the themes of abandonment and the need for companionship: Victor's mother adopted the abandoned Elizabeth because she herself was orphaned while still young.

The **third chapter** begins with the death of Victor's mother, who dies while successfully nursing Elizabeth from scarlet fever. On her deathbed, Victor's mother repeats that she hopes Victor and Elizabeth will marry when the time comes. After a brief period of mourning in which Elizabeth accepts responsibility for the household, Victor goes off to be educated at the university in Ingolstadt, Germany. He is seventeen when he leaves Elizabeth, his father, and his younger brothers. At the university Victor resumes his childhood interest in natural philosophy: his passion to divine the secrets of life and death is rekindled and he devotes himself completely to understanding chemistry.

In the following two years of study Victor advances quite rapidly and is recognized for his uncommon abilities in science. In **chapter four** he becomes interested in physiology, particularly the human body and the source of its life. "To examine the causes of life," Victor understood, "we must first have recourse to death." This realization leads him to study how the human body dies and decays. His research experiments should have repulsed him, he says, but he was driven to find an answer. After a time, it comes to him, and he is overwhelmed by the prospect that he alone may have discovered the secret of life and death. It is at this point that he determines to create a human being and invest it with life. With a zeal and determination that knows no limits, Victor works toward this end. He neglects his health and the letters from his family. Though in retelling his tale to Captain Walton Victor warns of "one who aspires to become greater than his nature will allow," at the time of his experiment excitement blinded him to such dangers and even caused him to believe he may be creating "a new species" that would "bless him" as their "creator and source."

Two more years pass before Victor finishes his project. In **chapter five** the creature awakes, but as soon as Victor sees "the dull yellow eye of the creature open" he is overcome with horror at what he has done and is unable to stand the creature's presence. Victor immediately flees his apartment. Tormented and frightened that the creature may be following, Victor wanders the night in dread. In the morning he happens to meet his friend Henry Clerval, who has just arrived at the university to study. Clerval quickly notices Victor's terrible state and his unwillingness to explain its cause. When they go back to Victor's apartment Victor is overjoyed to discover "the monster" he created has left. But Victor imagines that he sees it and that it tries to kill him. This hallucination is the start of a nervous breakdown that lasts many months. In **chapter six** Clerval nurses Victor back to health and Victor plans to return to his family in Geneva. It has been six years since he left them.

Chapters seven through nine describe the first series of tragedies that befall Victor as a result of his creation—or perhaps as a consequence for turning away from his creation, as the novel strongly suggests. Before Victor returns to Geneva his father writes to inform him that Victor's youngest brother, William, has been murdered. While rushing home to commiserate with his family, Victor catches a glimpse of the being he created, whom he had done his best to forget. As soon as he sees the giant deformed man running off and ascending the mountainous cliffs, Victor is certain the monster has killed William. Unfortunately, the murderer is believed to be Justine Moritz, a young girl who long ago had been taken in by Victor's father and mother and raised as a member of the family. Victor is united with his father and beloved Elizabeth, who is convinced Justine is innocent. However, the evidence against Justine is strong. The necklace that was stolen from the murdered boy and presumed to be the cause for the murder was discovered in Justine's pocket and she has no explanation for possessing it. At Justine's trial Elizabeth speaks on Justine's behalf and defends her innocence, but Justine is found guilty and condemned to death. Victor considers himself the murderer of both William and Justine and cannot endure the torment, but even in his exclamations of anguish he never tells of his creature or explains how he may be responsible for these tragedies.

Victor hopes to ease his sorrow by visiting the nearby mountains he enjoyed as a youth, but upon reaching the deserted summit alone (in **chapter ten**) Victor is approached by the being he has created. Victor is filled with rage and threatens to kill the "abhorred monster" for the deaths of William and Justine. Frankenstein's creation is not surprised by Victor's reception and responds woefully: "All men hate the wretched; how, then, must I be hated, who am miserable beyond all living things!" Unmoved by his pleas, Victor again threatens his creation, who continues to beg for compassion. "Remember that I am thy creature," he pleads. "I ought to be thy Adam, but am rather the fallen angel, whom thou drivest from joy for no misdeed." Victor at last is moved enough to listen to "the monster's" request. "For the first time," he admits, "I felt what the duties of a creator towards his creature were."

Frankenstein's creation tells his harrowing tale in **chapters eleven through seventeen.** After "awaking" to life and leaving Victor Frankenstein's laboratory, the creature remembers walking to some nearby woods, where he is able to quench his thirst in a natural brook and take the edge off his hunger by eating some berries. Over the next few days the creature "discovers" the sun and the moon and, more importantly, a campfire. He decides to leave the woods in pursuit of more food and comes upon a shepherd's hut and enters. An old man eating breakfast flees in horror at the creature's size and deformity. After eating the man's breakfast and sleeping in the bed of straw, the creature wanders into the village. He is amazed by the well-built cottages and plentiful gardens but is quickly surrounded by the villagers and stoned and chased. He escapes the mob and hides in a small hut connected to a cottage. Though confused and badly wounded, he is happy to have found shelter from the weather, "and still more from the barbarity of man."

It so happens that the monster is able to see into the cottage interior from a small hole in his little shelter. Through this hole Frankenstein's creation is able to observe the French family inside without being detected. The family consists of an old blind man, De Lacey, and his grown children, Agatha and Felix. Since Frankenstein's creature has never before seen human kindness, he is moved by the family's love for one another and longs to be among them, though he dare not approach them for fear of scaring them and losing what little connection he has with them. In an effort to help the impoverished family, the monster gathers wood for them during the night. After a time, Felix's fiancée, Safie, appears at the cottage and joins the family. Since she is Turkish she cannot speak French, and when the cottagers teach her the language, Frankenstein's creation learns as well. Around this time he also learns to read by luckily coming across some books left in the nearby woods—Goethe's *The Sorrows of Young Werther,* Milton's *Paradise Lost,* and Plutarch's *Lives.* The creature's knowledge of human history and experience is greatly increased, but so is his awareness of the extremes of human cruelty and suffering. While reading *Paradise Lost* (an excerpt from which Mary Shelley used as an epigraph to her novel), Frankenstein's creation sees himself as a banished and fallen angel, with the exception that even Satan had his followers and companions but he, a solitary wretch, is doomed to be utterly alone.

Eventually the creature works up the courage to approach the kind old father De Lacey while the rest of the cottagers are out. Since the old man is blind he will not fear the monster's physical deformity. De Lacey listens sympathetically to the monster's pleas to be accepted, for he hears the honesty in the creature's voice. But before the creature can finish his plea, the old man's children return. They are horrified by the creature and chase him from the cottage. The creature retreats to the woods, where he passes the night in violent anguish and despair. He decides to revisit the old man again and reveal himself to the rest of the family only when they can see beyond his grotesque appearance. But when he returns to his hut adjoining the cottage he discovers the De Laceys have taken their meager belongings and left. He will never have another chance at being accepted and loved. This injustice infuriates him and he burns the cottage. Thoughts of revenge become his only solace and he determines to seek his creator, Victor Frankenstein. After a long journey to Geneva the creature comes upon an innocent child in the woods. Thinking the child would be too young and pure to be contaminated by prejudice, the creature approaches him in the hope of making a friend. But the boy recoils in horror and shouts that the demon must let him go or his father will punish him. In the struggle the monster discovers that the child is a member of the Frankenstein family. "You belong to my enemy," says the creature, and, in an effort to silence the shrieking child, strangles him in an instant. The monster notices the necklace on the boy's neck and takes it. Later that night he comes upon Justine Moritz sleeping in a barn and he places the necklace in her pocket in a deliberate attempt to incriminate her. Thus ending his tale of misery, the creature demands that Victor create a companion for him, another being like him.

Chapter seventeen rehashes the dramatic argument between Victor Frankenstein and his creature concerning the creature's demand to have a female companion. During parts of the creature's long tale Victor had been moved to sympathy, but hearing again of his brother's murder and seeing the inhuman strength of the creature before him make Victor deny the creature's request. "I am malicious because I am miserable," the creature explains. He will not give up hope for companionship and begs Victor for a mate. "Oh! My creator, make me happy; let me feel gratitude towards you for one benefit! Let me see that I excite the sympathy of some existing thing." If Victor complies, the monster promises to go with his mate to the jungles of South America never again to be seen by human beings. At length, Victor is persuaded and agrees to create a companion for the creature. The monster says he will follow Victor and appear when the companion creature is ready; before Victor can change his mind, the creature runs off and vanishes.

Chapters eighteen through twenty chronicle Victor's progress and feelings while constructing a second being. Victor returns to his family with heavy heart and is unable to start the wretched task before him. He hides his anguish from his father, who considers Victor fully recovered from his previous suffering. Victor's father restates that he looks forward with great hope to Victor's marriage to Elizabeth and asks whether Victor's dark moods had been caused by an unwillingness to marry her. Victor proclaims his faithful and unswerving love for his dear Elizabeth but offers a phony excuse to postpone the marriage until after he has completed the companion creature he must make. Victor travels with his friend Henry Clerval to England, where Victor has access to the latest scientific discoveries. With a foreboding sense of evil and despair, he travels alone to a remote part of Scotland for the isolation he needs to complete his "unearthly occupation." Late one night in his lab close to the completion of the second creation Victor is overcome with fear and revulsion. What if this second creature does not agree to flee from humanity? What if she also is repulsed by the deformities of Frankenstein's first creation? Worse still would be the inhuman children the two creatures may have and unleash upon the world. Frankenstein looks up to see his first wretched creature peering in at the window. In a fit of rage Victor tears apart the being he had been constructing. Upon seeing his only hopes for happiness destroyed, the monster vows revenge and warns Victor, "I will be with you on your wedding-night."

The catalogue of the creature's revenge begins again in **chapter twenty-one.** Victor is briefly lost at sea after he dumps the remains of the second creature overboard. When he comes back to land he is surrounded and brought to the magistrate as a murder suspect. When he learns that a man had been strangled the night he was lost at sea he recalls that his creation had strangled his brother William. But Victor is not prepared to discover that the man just murdered is his dear friend Henry Clerval. In horror he exclaims that he is responsible and collapses in convulsions. For the next two months Victor lies delirious with fever in a prison cell. Upon his convalescence Victor is visited by his father. Victor's innocence in the murder is proved by eyewitnesses who attest to his being elsewhere when Clerval was murdered. Victor and his father return to Geneva.

In **chapter twenty-two** Victor and Elizabeth are married. As he pledges himself to Elizabeth, Victor remembers the threat the monster made to him: "I will be with you on your wedding-night." He remains agitated and vigilant and tells Elizabeth that he will share the secret of all his past despair on the day after their wedding. In the meantime he expects his fight to the death with the "demon" he created with his own hands. However, in **chapter twenty-three,** while standing guard outside Elizabeth's bedroom on his wedding night, Victor hears Elizabeth scream in horror. It is at that moment that the truth of the monster's threat comes to him. He rushes in to the bedroom to find Elizabeth strangled. The monster had intended all along to kill his beloved Elizabeth and not him, as Victor had believed. Victor sees the fiendish grin of the creature looking in from the window. He draws his pistol, but the monster eludes him and escapes the crowd that hunts after him. Victor collapses and returns again to his aging father in Geneva, but the old man cannot endure the shock and dies within a few days. Victor again sinks into delirium and for many months is confined to a solitary cell. When he returns to his senses he reveals the whole secret of his unnatural creation to the magistrate in order to instigate a search for the murderer of William, Clerval, and Elizabeth, but it is clear that the tale is too fantastic to be believed and nothing comes of Victor's entreaties.

The final chapter of the novel, **chapter twenty-four,** brings us to the end of Victor Frankenstein's narration. He explains how, with nothing left and no ties to human life, he has devoted himself to the sole task of finding his creation and killing it. In the never-ending hunt Victor consequently lives as miserable and lonely an existence as the cast-off being he hunts. Despite fatigue and hunger, he pursues the monster's trail, sometimes being told of the creature's whereabouts from villagers, sometimes following clues left tauntingly by the creature himself. Occasionally the creature also leaves food for Victor to ensure that he will not give up or die before the two have a chance to meet again and wrestle for their lives. Victor follows his hated creation to the icy climes of the Arctic until he loses sight of him. It was at this point that Captain Walton discovered Victor floating on the block of ice and rescued him. Having thus finished his tale, Victor stops himself from asking Captain Walton to join him in his hunt for the monster, but he does request that Walton kill the monster if he encounters it after Victor has died.

Walton now resumes the narration and writes his sister that all is not well with his expedition. Frankenstein has fallen gravely ill and the ship is in danger from ice encroaching on all sides. Walton laments that he may lose his only friend. The ship's predicament worsens and the ship's crew demands that the expedition be aborted. They wish to return home to safety, if possible, but, surprisingly, Victor Frankenstein delivers a speech of courage and heroism that overcomes their fears temporarily. But shortly thereafter Captain Walton consents to call off his expedition, though he cannot bear leaving his dreams for glory and discovery unsatisfied. Victor Frankenstein, however, will not give up his quest so easily. He tries to get out of bed but collapses, close to death. His dying words to Walton are: "Seek happiness in tranquillity and avoid ambition."

After Victor dies Walton hears sounds coming from the cabin where Victor's body lies. Upon entering the cabin Walton sees the giant being, "the monster," whom Victor created. The creature is overwrought with grief and begs the dead Victor for forgiveness. Walton scolds the creature for his path of destruction, yet the creature speaks eloquently of being driven to evil by his own suffering and resentment for being permanently barred from companionship. "Am I to be thought the only criminal, when all humankind sinned against me?" the creature asks. We are reminded of the creature's earnest hopes to live in peace and love with the De Lacey family in the cottage. Despite the injustices of forever being "spurned at, and kicked, and trampled on," the creature recognizes his own guilt and is penitent for the murders he committed. "You hate me," the creature tells Walton, "but your abhorrence cannot equal that with which I regard myself." After this admission the creature promises to flee to the North Pole, where he will end his wretchedness forever by burning himself alive. The creature leaves the cabin and Walton watches him float off on the ice into the dark distance. ✤

—Michael R. Steinberg
New York University

List of Characters

Victor Frankenstein is very different from the evil mad scientist of most movie portrayals of Frankenstein. The young man who discovers how to piece together a man and reanimate the body with the spark of life is a sensitive though driven character. His greatest faults are his intellectual and scientific ambition to pierce the secrets of nature and his uncaring abandonment of his creation: after bringing his creature to life he flees from it in horror. Never accepting his responsibility, Victor casts off the creature as a wretched, deformed monster. Briefly Victor is moved to produce a companion being for his creature, but he refuses to complete it for fear the two would cause greater evil. Consequently the monster seeks revenge on Frankenstein by murdering Frankenstein's friends and family. In turn Frankenstein devotes his life to hunting and killing his creation. Though Victor Frankenstein is not always characterized sympathetically, Captain Walton remains very impressed by his earnestness.

Frankenstein's creation, whom Victor Frankenstein calls "the wretch," "the demon," and "the monster," is also very different from most portrayals in movies. Though a giant man of grotesque proportions, the creation at heart is well-intentioned and gentle. He longs to be accepted by humans and hopes to live among them, but he is repeatedly beaten and chased away because of his appearance. For a time he is able to live undetected alongside a cottage in which a loving but impoverished family lives. The creature is deeply moved by their tenderness and wants nothing more than to join the family in devotion, but again he is chased away. Eternal loneliness and misery at the hands of human cruelty drive the creature to malicious revenge upon his creator. Still, despite "the monster's" vengeful murders, it has been said that the creature is more human than his creator. Though his path of destruction eventually includes the death of Victor Frankenstein, his creator, the monster ultimately finds no solace from his misery and guilt and determines to kill himself.

Elizabeth Lavenza is called Victor Frankenstein's cousin because she was adopted by Victor's mother while still a little girl. She and Victor spend their childhood together and both look with joy toward the day they will be married. Just as Victor and his creation may be seen to represent the difference between intellect and emotions, so too do Victor and Elizabeth seem opposite in this regard. Elizabeth is characterized as pure, compassionate, and trusting, and she is entirely devoted to Victor and her family. She is murdered on her wedding night as part of Frankenstein's monster's revenge.

(Robert) Walton is the character who, in writing his sister during the course of his expedition to the North Pole, narrates the entire novel. Walton is most like Victor Frankenstein in that he has an overreaching quest for knowledge, especially an ambition to know the truths of nature, yet he does not recognize that his ambition endangers others (the ship's crew) as well as himself. But he is also like Frankenstein's creation in that he yearns for companionship and friendship, and feels this need most poignantly. It is left ambiguous what moral Walton learns from hearing of the tragedies that Victor Frankenstein's irresponsible ambition brought him or from meeting the doomed creature Frankenstein abandoned.

Alphonse Frankenstein is Victor's father. Throughout the novel he is shown to be caring and supportive of his family. He repeatedly tries to help Victor overcome his sorrows, though he never learns the true source of his son's anguish.

(Henry) Clerval is Victor Frankenstein's devoted friend. As children, while Victor was fascinated by science and natural philosophy, it was human society, ethics, and morality that interested Clerval. Their friendship also exemplifies the distinction between head and heart. Clerval is finally able to convince his father of the importance of a liberal arts education—even to one in business—but when he arrives at the university in Ingolstadt to study he selflessly devotes many months to nursing his friend Victor Frankenstein back to health, since Victor has collapsed from the turmoil and horror of making his creature. After the deaths of William and Justine, Clerval tries to cheer Victor by escorting him on his trip to Scotland (where Victor planned to make his second creature). Frankenstein's monster kills Clerval after Victor refuses to honor his promise to make the creature a companion.

William Frankenstein is Victor's youngest brother and the first victim of Frankenstein's monster's revenge.

Justine Moritz is the young girl who is wrongly condemned to death for the murder of William. She had lived like a sister with the Frankenstein family.

The old man De Lacey and his daughter Agatha and son Felix are the family that Frankenstein's creature observes while living in the hut cottage adjoining their cottage. It is by watching and listening to this family that the creature learns to speak. Though originally wealthy, the family has become impoverished as a consequence of someone else's greed and treachery. Yet, to the creature's innocent eyes, the family is rich with love and human dignity. When the grown children become despondent, their blind father plays his guitar to soothe them. Frankenstein's creature is also deeply moved by this. The creature longs to join them and share their warmth and he secretly aids them in their chores. At last he approaches the blind father when the children are away. The old man listens sympathetically as the monster begs to be understood and accepted, but before he can finish the others return and in fear and horror chase him away. The De Laceys leave the cottage and again the monster is abandoned. ❖

Critical Views

[Sir Walter Scott (1771–1832), known primarily as a novelist, poet, and dramatist, was also an important critic and essayist. He contributed literary reviews and essays to the *Edinburgh Review,* the *Quarterly Review,* and the *Encyclopaedia Britannica,* and he wrote biographies of John Dryden (1808) and Jonathan Swift (1814) when editing their collected works. In the following review of *Frankenstein,* Scott praises the author's ability to tell such a fantastic and unnerving tale in clear, precise language.]

It is no slight merit in our eyes, that the tale ⟨*Frankenstein*⟩, though wild in incident, is written in plain and forcible English, without exhibiting that mixture of hyperbolical Germanisms with which tales of wonder are usually told, as if it were necessary that the language should be as extravagant as the fiction. The ideas of the author are always clearly as well as forcibly expressed; and his descriptions of landscape have in them the choice requisites of truth, freshness, precision, and beauty. The self-education of the monster, considering the slender opportunities of acquiring knowledge that he possessed, we have already noticed as improbable and overstrained. That he should not only have learned to speak, but to read, and, for aught we know, to write—that he should have become acquainted with *Werter,* with *Plutarch's Lives,* and with *Paradise Lost,* by listening through a hole in the wall, seems as unlikely as that he should have acquired, in the same way, the problems of *Euclid,* or the art of book-keeping by single and double entry. The author has however two apologies—the first, the necessity that his monster should acquire those endowments, and the other, that his neighbours were engaged in teaching the language of the country to a young foreigner. His progress in self-knowledge, and the acquisition of information is, after all, more wonderful than that of *Hai Eben Yokhdan,* or *Automathes,* or the hero of the little romance called *The Child of Nature,* one of which works might perhaps suggest the train of ideas followed by the author of *Frankenstein.* We should also be disposed, in support of the principles with which we set out, to question whether the monster, how tall, agile, and strong however, could have perpetrated so much mischief undiscovered; or passed through so many countries without being secured, either on account of his crimes, or for the benefit of some such speculator such as Mr Polito, who would have been happy to add to his museum so curious a specimen of natural history. But as we have consented to admit the leading incident of the work, perhaps some of our readers may be of the opinion, that to stickle upon lesser improbabilities, is to incur the censure bestowed by the Scottish proverb on those who "start at straws, after swallowing *windlings.*"

—Sir Walter Scott, "Remarks on *Frankenstein; or, The Modern Prometheus,*" *Blackwood's Edinburgh Magazine* 2, No. 12 (March 1818): 619

Percy Bysshe Shelley on the Moral Significance of *Frankenstein*

[Percy Bysshe Shelley (1792–1822), the husband of Mary Shelley and an important member of the English Romantic school of poetry, showed an interest in the supernatural as early as his days at Oxford University, where he wrote two Gothic novels. In this enthusiastic review of *Frankenstein* (not published during his lifetime), Shelley comments on the moral nature of the novel.]

The novel of *Frankenstein; or, The Modern Prometheus,* is undoubtedly, as a mere story, one of the most original and complete productions of the day. We debate with ourselves in wonder, as we read it, what could have been the series of thoughts—what could have been the peculiar experiences that awakened them—which conduced, in the author's mind, to the astonishing combinations of motives and incidents, and the startling catastrophe, which compose this tale. There are, perhaps, some points of subordinate importance, which prove that it is the author's first attempt. But in this judgment, which requires a very nice discrimination, we may be mistaken; for it is conducted throughout with a firm and steady hand. The interest gradually accumulates and advances towards the conclusion with the accelerated rapidity of a rock rolled down a mountain. We are led breathless with suspense and sympathy, and the heaping up of incident on incident, and the working of passion out of passion. We cry "hold, hold! enough!"—but there is yet something to come; and, like the victim whose history it relates, we think we can bear no more, and yet more is to be borne. Pelion is heaped on Ossa, and Ossa on Olympus. We climb Alp after Alp, until the horizon is seen blank, vacant, and limitless; and the head turns giddy, and the ground seems to fail under our feet.

This novel rests its claim on being a source of powerful and profound emotion. The elementary feelings of the human mind are exposed to view; and those who are accustomed to reason deeply on their origin and tendency will, perhaps, be the only persons who can sympathize, to the full extent, in the interest of the actions which are their result. But, founded on nature as they are, there is perhaps no reader, who can endure anything beside a new love-story, who will not feel a responsive string touched in his inmost soul. The sentiments are so affectionate and so innocent—the characters of the subordinate agents in this strange drama are clothed in the light of such a mild and gentle mind—the pictures of domestic manners are of the most simple and attaching character: the pathos is irresistible and deep. Nor are the crimes and malevolence of the single Being, though indeed withering and tremendous, the offspring of any unaccountable propensity to evil, but flow irresistibly from certain causes fully adequate to their production. They are the children, as it were, of Necessity and Human Nature. In this the direct moral of the book consists; and it is perhaps the most important, and of the most universal application, of any moral that can be enforced by example. Treat a person ill, and he will become wicked. Requite affection with scorn;—let one being be selected, for whatever cause, as the refuse of his kind—divide him, a social being, from society, and you impose upon him the irresistible obligations—malevolence and selfishness. It is thus that, too often in society, those who are best qualified to be its benefactors and its ornaments are branded by some accident with scorn, and changed, by neglect and solitude of heart, into a scourge and a curse.

The Being in "Frankenstein" is, no doubt, a tremendous creature. It was impossible that he should not have received among men that treatment which led to the consequences of his being a social nature. He was an abortion and an anomaly; and though his mind was such as its first impressions framed it, affectionate and full of moral sensibility, yet the circumstances of his existence are so monstrous and uncommon, that, when the consequences of them became developed in action, his original goodness was gradually turned into inextinguishable misanthropy and revenge. The scene between the Being and the blind De Lacey in the cottage is one of the most profound and extraordinary instances of pathos that we ever recollect. It is impossible to read this dialogue,—and indeed many others of a somewhat similar character,—without feeling the heart suspend its pulsations with wonder, and the "tears stream down the cheeks." The encounter and argument between Frankenstein and the Being on the sea of ice, almost approaches, in effect, to the expostulation of Caleb Williams with Falkland. It reminds us, indeed, somewhat of the style and character of that admirable writer, to whom the author has dedicated his work, and whose productions he seems to have studied.

There is only one instance, however, in which we detect the least approach to imitation; and that is the conduct of the incident of Frankenstein's landing in Ireland. The general character of the tale, indeed, resembles nothing that ever preceded it. After the death of Elizabeth, the story, like a stream which grows at once more rapid and profound as it proceeds, assumes an irresistible solemnity, and the magnificent energy and swiftness of a tempest.

The churchyard scene, in which Frankenstein visits the tombs of his family, his quitting Geneva, and his journey through Tartary to the shores of the Frozen Ocean, resemble at once the terrible reanimation of a corpse and the supernatural career of a spirit. The scene in the cabin of Walton's ship—the more than mortal enthusiasm and grandeur of the Being's speech over the dead body of his victim—is an exhibition of intellectual and

imaginative power, which we think the reader will acknowl-
edge has seldom been surpassed.

—Percy Bysshe Shelley, "On *Frankenstein*" (1818), *The Complete Works of Percy Bysshe Shelley*, ed. Roger Ingpen and Walter E. Peck (New York: Scribner's 1926–30), Vol. 6, pp. 263–65

Mary Shelley on the Writing of *Frankenstein*

[*Frankenstein* was originally published in 1818 anonymously. After it achieved success, Mary Shelley openly
acknowledged its authorship and, in this introduction
to a reprint of the novel, spoke of the circumstances
under which it was written.]

In the summer of 1816 we visited Switzerland and became the
neighbours of Lord Byron. At first we spent our pleasant hours
on the lake or wandering on its shores; and Lord Byron, who
was writing the third canto of *Childe Harold,* was the only one
among us who put his thoughts upon paper. These, as he
brought them successively to us, clothed in all the light and
harmony of poetry, seemed to stamp as divine the glories of
heaven and earth, whose influences we partook with him. ⟨. . .⟩

"We will each write a ghost story," said Lord Byron, and his
proposition was acceded to. There were four of us. The noble
author began a tale, a fragment of which he printed at the end
of his poem of Mazeppa. Shelley, more apt to embody ideas
and sentiments in the radiance of brilliant imagery and in the
music of the most melodious verse that adorns our language
than to invent the machinery of a story, commenced one
founded on the experiences of his early life. Poor Polidori had
some terrible idea about a skull-headed lady who was so pun-
ished for peeping through a key-hole—what to see I forget:
something very shocking and wrong of course; but when she
was reduced to a worse condition than the renowned Tom
of Coventry, he did not know what to do with her and was

obliged to dispatch her to the tomb of the Capulets, the only place for which she was fitted. The illustrious poets also, annoyed by the platitude of prose, speedily relinquished their uncongenial task.

I busied myself *to think of a story*—a story to rival those which had excited us to this task. One which would speak to the mysterious fears of our nature and awaken thrilling horror—one to make the reader dread to look round, to curdle the blood, and quicken the beatings of the heart. If I did not accomplish these things, my ghost story would be unworthy of its name. I thought and pondered—vainly. I felt that blank incapability of invention which is the greatest misery of authorship, when dull Nothing replies to our anxious invocations. "Have you thought of a story?" I was asked each morning, and each morning I was forced to reply with a mortifying negative. ⟨. . .⟩

Night waned upon this talk, and even the witching hour had gone by before we retired to rest. When I placed my head on my pillow I did not sleep, nor could I be said to think. My imagination, unbidden, possessed and guided me, gifting the successive images that arose in my mind with a vividness far beyond the usual bounds of reverie. I saw—with shut eyes, but acute mental vision—I saw the pale student of unhallowed arts kneeling beside the thing he had put together. I saw the hideous phantasm of a man stretched out, and then, on the working of some powerful engine, show signs of life and stir with an uneasy, half-vital motion. Frightful must it be, for supremely frightful would be the effect of any human endeavour to mock the stupendous mechanism of the Creator of the world. His success would terrify the artist; he would rush away from his odious handiwork, horror-stricken. He would hope that, left to itself, the slight spark of life which he had communicated would fade, that this thing which had received such imperfect animation would subside into dead matter, and he might sleep in the belief that the silence of the grave would quench forever the transient existence of the hideous corpse which he had looked upon as the cradle of life. He sleeps; but he is awakened; he opens his eyes; behold, the horrid thing stands at his bedside, opening his curtains and looking on him with yellow, watery, but speculative eyes.

I opened mine in terror. The idea so possessed my mind that a thrill of fear ran through me, and I wished to exchange the ghastly image of my fancy for the realities around. I see them still: the very room, the dark parquet, the closed shutters with the moonlight struggling through, and the sense I had that the glassy lake and white high Alps were beyond. I could not so easily get rid of my hideous phantom; still it haunted me. I must try to think of something else. I recurred to my ghost story—my tiresome, unlucky ghost story! Oh! If I could only contrive one which would frighten my reader as I myself had been frightened that night!

Swift as light and as cheering was the idea that broke in upon me. "I have found it! What terrified me will terrify others; and I need only describe the spectre which had haunted my midnight pillow." On the morrow I announced that I had *thought of a story.*

—Mary Shelley, "Author's Introduction" (1831), *Frankenstein; or, The Modern Prometheus* (New York: Modern Library, 1993), pp. xv–xx

Helen Moore on *Frankenstein* as Allegory

[Helen Moore is the author of *Mary Wollstonecraft Shelley* (1886), from which the following extract is taken. Here, Moore maintains that *Frankenstein* is compelling because of the subtle allegory infusing it, especially the notion of discarding the established order of things, a guiding force in the thought of Percy Bysshe Shelley.]

Regarded as a mere tale, it is difficult to account for the hold this story has always had upon the minds of the reading world. As a story it does not justify its own success. To say that it is remarkable as a work of imagination does not meet the difficulty. By a work of the imagination, as used in the current criticism of *Frankenstein,* is simply meant that it is a fantastic romance, such as we find in the *Arabian Nights,* or in the prose tales of Poe. But a position utterly different from these is accorded to *Frankenstein.*

We have intimated that there was a dual quality in it, to which it owed its singular power and place in literature. One element is doubtless the horror of the tale and the weird fancy of the author's imagination in the ordinary acceptation of the word. But it is to an entirely different department of mental conception that we must look for the secret of its peculiar influence. The faculty of imagination is something more than the recalling and rearrangements of past impressions. Profoundly considered, it is that function of the mind which formulates, as though real, a state of things which if present would so appear. It is the power of projecting the mind into unhappened realities. It is the faculty of picturing unseen verities. There is thus in it a prophetic element, not at all miraculous, but dependent upon subtle laws of association and suggestion. It is to this element that *Frankenstein* owes its power over thoughtful minds. It is by virtue of the allegorical element in it that it holds its high position as a work of the imagination. Yet so unobtrusively is the allegory woven through the thread of the romance, that, while always felt, it can scarcely be said to have been detected. Certain it is that no one has directed attention to this phase, or carefully attempted an analysis of the work, with the view of deducing the meaning thus legible between the lines.

That Mrs. Shelley herself was conscious of this element is certain, by the double title she gave it,—*Frankenstein, or the Modern Prometheus.* Furthermore, that she should thus embody, under the apparent guise of a weird story, suggestions of moral truths, development of mental traits,—normal and abnormal,—and hints at, and solutions of, social questions, was in strict accord both with her own intellectual state and with the circumstances under which *Frankenstein* was produced. And yet nothing is more improbable than that it was written with such design, or that the youthful author was fully aware or even conscious of the extent to which the allegorical overlies largely the narrative in her work. This very unconsciousness of result, this obliviousness to hidden truths, is a distinguishing mark of genius. To take daily account of stock proclaims the small trader, not the merchant prince. Placed in a congenial atmosphere, genius in breathing the breath of life will exhale truths. The very gist of genius is embodied in this hidden relation to truth. That mind has genius which, detecting germs of truth under forms where the common eye sees them not, affords in itself the place and pabulum for their growth.⟨...⟩

But the chief allegorical interest in the narrative concerns itself about that tendency in the human being to discard the established order of things and to create for itself a new and independent existence. In the simple story, Frankenstein made a being responsible to him alone for its creation,—a being not produced by the ordinary course of life, not amenable or even adaptable to the existing world of men. Right or wrong, better or worse, the creature may be, but different certainly, and this irreconcilable disparity points back ever to its origin, which had been anomalous and strange.

The whole story is but the elaboration of the embarrassment and dangers which flow from departure from the ordinary course of nature; this forced attempt to invade society from within. What strong existence in real life of this same tendency Mary Shelley had seen in those nearest and dearest to her! She has not failed to learn the lesson of her mother's history; time analyzes rather than destroys. And the life of Mary Wollstonecraft was doubtless seen by the clear-minded daughter in stronger contrast of light and shade than it had been by its contemporaries. Who knew so well the glories of that life? Its successes as well as its miseries had sprung from the self-same causes as those of Frankenstein,—from the breach of the conventional; from overstepping the limits; from creating an individuality and a sphere of existence denied it by Nomos, and consequently sure of the hostility of society.

To this same cause Shelley himself attributed justly the events and moral struggle of his own life. From earliest childhood revolt against convention, and rebellion against authority, had characterized him. His perpetual tendency, like that of Mary Wollstonecraft, like that typified in *Frankenstein,* was ever to create for himself an existence not conforming to the ways of the world.

As we read the story of the modern Prometheus, and page by page trace the evolution of this idea, the ethical aspect is oppressive in its prophetic truth. Each must do this for himself. One thing, however, we may note. The visitation of judgment, the terrible results of the exercise of the power of creation, do not begin, do not recoil upon Frankenstein, until he has actually launched his creature into the world of men about him. So long as he kept the scheme within himself; so long as the influence of the thought and work was confined to him alone, no evil came; on the contrary, after a certain point the struggle after this ideal was a stimulation and an incentive of the highest order. It was only when the overt act of introducing his new existence into the world was accomplished, that misery began to flow from it to all concerned, and even to those apparently not concerned in it. This is the saving clause in the prophetic allegory. Without this it would fail to square with the truth.

See how far-reaching are the ideas which this allegory evokes, how subtle its suggestions are. Mind after mind has felt the power of this story, so simple in its apparent construction, and has again and again returned to it, not asking itself why; feeling a power it did not recognize, much less analyze; hovering, in fact, around it as birds do when charmed, because of an attraction which was persistent and real, although unknown, even unsuspected. All attraction implies some sort of a magnet. Nothing attracts so powerfully as the true.
—Helen Moore, *Mary Wollstonecraft Shelley* (Philadelphia: J. B. Lippincott Co., 1886), pp. 248–50, 254–56

EDITH BIRKHEAD ON THE STRUCTURE OF *FRANKENSTEIN*

[Edith Birkhead is the author of a notable critical work, *The Tale of Terror* (1921), a pioneering study of the Gothic novel. In this extract from that work, Birkhead finds the structure of *Frankenstein* to be awkward in its profusion of documents and believes that the work would have been better as a short story.]

Like *Alastor, Frankenstein* was a plea for human sympathy, and was, according to Shelley's preface, intended "to exhibit the amiableness of domestic affection and the excellence of universal virtue." The monster has the perception and desire of goodness, but, by the circumstances of his abnormal existence, is delivered over to evil. It is this dual nature that prevents him from being a mere automaton. The monster indeed is far more real than the shadowy beings whom he pursues. Frankenstein is less an individual than a type, and only interests us through the emotions which his conflict with the monster arouses. Clerval, Elizabeth and Frankenstein's relatives are passive sufferers whose psychology does not concern us. Mrs. Shelley rightly lavishes her skill on the central figure of the book, and succeeds, as effectually as Frankenstein himself, in infusing into him the spark of life. Mrs. Shelley's aim is to "awaken thrilling horror," and, incidentally, to "exhibit the excellence of domestic virtue," and for her purpose the demon is of paramount importance. The involved, complex plot of a novel seemed to pass beyond Mrs. Shelley's control. A short tale she could handle successfully, and Shelley was unwise in inciting her to expand *Frankenstein* into a long narrative. So long as she is completely carried away by her subject Mrs. Shelley writes clearly, but when she pauses to regard the progress of her story dispassionately, she seems to be overwhelmed by the wealth of her resources and to have no power of selecting the relevant details. The laborious introductory letters, the meticulous record of Frankenstein's education, the story of Felix and Sofie, the description of the tour through England before the creation of the second monster is attempted, are all connected with the main theme by very frail links and serve to distract our attention in an irritating fashion from what really interests us. In the novel of mystery a tantalising delay may be singularly effective. In a novel which depends chiefly for its effect on sheer horror, delays are merely dangerous. By resting her terrors on a pseudo-scientific basis and by placing her story in a definite locality, Mrs. Shelley waives her right to an entire suspension of disbelief. If it be reduced to its lowest terms, the plot of Frankenstein, with its bewildering confusion of the prosaic and the fantastic, sounds as crude, disjointed and inconsequent as that of a nightmare. Mrs. Shelley's timid hesitation between imagination and reality, her attempt to reconcile incompatible things and to place a creature who belongs to no earthly land in familiar surroundings, prevents *Frankenstein* from being a wholly satisfactory and alarming novel of terror. She loves the fantastic, but she also fears it. She is weighted down by commonsense, and so flutters instead of soaring, unwilling to trust herself far from the material world. But the fact that she was able to vivify her grotesque skeleton of a plot with some degree of success is no mean tribute to her gifts. The energy and vigour of her style, her complete and serious absorption in her subject, carry us safely over many an absurdity. It is only in the duller stretches of the narrative, when her heart is not in her work, that her language becomes vague, indeterminate and blurred, and that she muffles her thoughts in words like "ascertain," "commencement," "peruse," "diffuse," instead of using their simpler Saxon equivalents. Stirred by the excitement of the events she describes, she can write forcibly in simple, direct language. She often frames short, hurried sentences such as a man would naturally utter when breathless with terror or with recollections of terror. The final impression that *Frankenstein* leaves with us is not easy to define, because the book is so uneven in quality. It is obviously the shapeless work of an immature writer who has had no experience in evolving a plot. Sometimes it is genuinely moving and impressive, but it continually falls abruptly and ludicrously short of its aim. Yet when all its faults have been laid bare, the fact remains that few readers would abandon the story half-way through. Mrs. Shelley is so thoroughly engrossed in her theme that she impels her readers onward, even though they may think but meanly of her story as a work of art.

—Edith Birkhead, *The Tale of Terror: A Study of the Gothic Romance* (London: Constable, 1921), pp. 163–65

[Elizabeth Nitchie is the author of *The Criticism of Literature* (1928) and *Mary Shelley: Author of* Frankenstein (1953), from which the following extract is taken. Here, Nitchie argues that Mary Shelley's psychological need for companionship and her personal understanding of loneliness underlie the solitary condition of the monster in *Frankenstein*.]

Out of one of the happiest periods of her life came her most remarkable study of loneliness. *Frankenstein* is far more than a horror story based on presumptuous experiments in chemistry and biology. Its two themes of scientific curiosity and of loneliness run parallel to each other. Each is foreshadowed in the person of Robert Walton, the explorer whose curiosity about the North Pole is carrying him to the solitary ice fields of the Arctic regions. In the story itself, one becomes the motive of Frankenstein's life, the other the tragic fate of his monstrous creation. Here too are the symbols of solitude: Walton's solitary childhood, his lack of a friend on board his ship, the deserted graveyards, Frankenstein's lonely laboratory, the valleys of Servox and Chamounix, Mont Blanc dwelling apart, Montanvert "terrifically desolate," the isolated hut on "the remotest of the Orkneys," the ship caught in the endless fields of ice, the single dog-sled, the figure of the Monster disappearing into the unpeopled north.

The Monster, central symbol of loneliness, yearning for human intercourse, was set apart by the circumstances of his origin and by his deformity. There was always a barrier before him, like the wall which separated him in his hovel from the DeLaceys in their warm, social cottage. His every attempt to pass this barrier, to help others or to win affection, was repulsed with fear and horror. When Frankenstein, repenting of his reluctant promise to fashion a mate for him, tore his work apart, the Monster was doomed to a life of solitude and therefore of crime: his generous motives were changed to a desire for revenge on his creator and on the whole human race. "Evil thenceforth became my good," he said to Walton over the dead body of Frankenstein, ". . . the fallen angel becomes a malignant devil. Yet even that enemy of God and man had friends and associates in his desolation; I am alone." That this monstrous being could be imagined by a young girl is due partly to the fact that he is the symbol of her own loneliness.

—Elizabeth Nitchie, *Mary Shelley: Author of* Frankenstein (New Brunswick, NJ: Rutgers University Press, 1953), pp. 16–17

HAROLD BLOOM ON ROMANTIC MYTHOLOGY IN *FRANKENSTEIN*

[Harold Bloom (b. 1930), one of the leading literary critics of the century, is Sterling Professor of the Humanities at Yale University and Henry W. and Albert A. Berg Professor of English at the New York University Graduate School. Among his most important volumes are *The Anxiety of Influence* (1973) and *The Western Canon* (1994). In the following extract, Bloom examines the significance of the Prometheus myth in *Frankenstein* and points to the novel's importance to Romantic writers.]

If we stand back from Mary Shelley's novel, in order better to view its archetypal shape, we see it as the quest of a solitary and ravaged consciousness first for consolation, then for revenge, and finally for a self-destruction that will be apocalyptic, that will bring down the creator with his creature. Though Mary Shelley may not have intended it, her novel's prime theme is a necessary counterpoise to Prometheanism, for Prometheanism exalts the increase in consciousness despite all cost. Frankenstein breaks through the barrier that separates man from God, and apparently becomes the giver of life, but all he actually can give is death-in-life. The profound dejection endemic in Mary Shelley's novel is fundamental to the Romantic mythology of the self, for all Romantic horrors are diseases of excessive consciousness, of the self unable to bear the self. Kierkegaard remarks that Satan's despair is absolute, because Satan as pure spirit is pure consciousness, and for

Satan (and all men in his predicament) every increase in consciousness is an increase in despair. Frankenstein's desperate creature attains the state of pure spirit through his extraordinary situation, and is racked by a consciousness in which every thought is a fresh disease.

A Romantic poet fought against self-consciousness through the strength of what he called imagination, a more than rational energy, by which thought could seek to heal itself. But Frankenstein's daemon, though he is in the archetypal situation of the Romantic Wanderer or Solitary, who sometimes was a poet, can win no release from his own story by telling it. His desperate desire for a mate is clearly an attempt to find a Shelleyan Epipsyche or Blakean Emanation for himself, a self within the self. But as he is the nightmare actualization of Frankenstein's desire, he is himself an emanation of Promethean yearnings, and his only double is his creator and denier.

When Coleridge's Ancient Mariner progressed from the purgatory of consciousness to his very minimal control of imagination, he failed to save himself. He remained in a cycle of remorse. But he at least became a salutary warning to others, and made of the Wedding Guest a wiser and better man. Frankenstein's creature can help neither himself nor others, for he has no natural ground to which he can return. Romantic poets liked to return to the imagery of the ocean of life and immortality; in the eddying to and fro of the healing waters they could picture a hoped-for process of restoration, of a survival of consciousness despite all its agonies. Mary Shelley, with marvelous appropriateness, brings her Romantic novel to a demonic conclusion in a world of ice. The frozen sea is the inevitable emblem for both the wretched daemon and his obsessed creator, but the daemon is allowed a final image of reversed Prometheanism. There is a heroism fully earned in the being who cries farewell in a claim of sad triumph: "I shall ascend my funeral pyre triumphantly, and exult in the agony of the torturing flames."

—Harold Bloom, "Frankenstein, or the New Prometheus," *Partisan Review* 32, No. 4 (Fall 1965): 617–18

[Brian W. Aldiss (b. 1925) is a prolific writer of science fiction who has written a sequel to *Frankenstein* entitled *Frankenstein Unbound* (1973). In the following extract from his history of science fiction, *Billion Year Spree* (1973), Aldiss notes that *Frankenstein* is a pioneering work of science fiction in its utilization of contemporary findings in science, notably galvanism and electricity.]

A reading of the novel reveals how precariously it is balanced between the old age and the new. In Chapter Three, Victor Frankenstein goes to university and visits two professors. To the first, a man called Krempe who is professor of natural philosophy, he reveals how his search for knowledge took him to the works of Cornelius Agrippa, Paracelsus, and Albertus Magnus. Krempe scoffs at him. "These fancies, which you have so greedily imbibed, are a thousand years old!" This is a modern objection; antiquity is no longer the highest court to which one can appeal.

Frankenstein attends the second professor, one Waldman, who lectures on chemistry. Waldman condemns the ancient teachers who "promised impossibilities, and performed nothing." He speaks instead of the moderns, who use microscope and crucible, and converts Frankenstein to his way of thinking. Symbolically, Frankenstein turns away from alchemy and the past towards science and the future—and is rewarded with his horrible success.

The hints in the novel as to how the "vital spark" is imparted in the composite body are elusive. In her Introduction to the 1831 edition, however, the author reveals the origins of her story. Like *The Castle of Otranto,* it began with a dream. In the dream, she saw "the hideous phantasm of a man stretched out, and then, on the working of some powerful engine, show signs of life, and stir with an uneasy, half vital motion." It was science fiction itself that stirred.

Greater events were stirring between the publication of the first and second editions of *Frankenstein.* The first volume of

Lyell's *Principles of Geology* had just appeared, drastically extending the age of the Earth. Mantell and others were grubbing gigantic fossil bones out of the ground, exhuming genera from the rocks as surely as Frankenstein's creature was patched together from various corpses. Already beginning was that great extension to our imaginative lives which we call the Age of Reptiles—those defunct monsters we have summoned back to vigorous existence.

Other references in the 1831 Introduction are to galvanism and electricity. The Preface to the first edition of 1818 is also instructive. Although Mary had set herself to write a ghost story, her intentions changed; she states expressly in the Preface, "I have not considered myself as merely weaving a series of supernatural terrors." The Preface is an apologia, and Mary Shelley's chief witness for her defence, mentioned in her first sentence, is Erasmus Darwin.

The sources of *Frankenstein* are documented. As Mary Shelley explains, her dream was inspired by late-night conversations with her husband, with Byron, and with Dr. Polidori. Their talk was of vampires and the supernatural; Polidori supplied the company with some suitable reading material; and Byron and Shelley also discussed Darwin, his thought and his experiments.

Mary's dream of a hideous phantasm stirring to life carries a reminder of a nightmare recorded in her journal a year earlier. In March 1815, she had just lost her first baby, born prematurely. On the fifteenth of the month, she wrote: "Dream that my little baby came to life again; that it had only been cold, and that we had rubbed it before the fire, and it had lived." In retrospect, the words have an eerie ring.

The Outwardness of Science and society is balanced, in the novel, by an Inwardness which Mary's dream helped her to accommodate. This particular balance is perhaps one of *Frankenstein*'s greatest merits: that its tale of exterior adventure and misfortune is always accompanied by a psychological depth.

—Brian W. Aldiss, Billion Year Spree: The True History of Science Fiction (Garden City, NY: Doubleday, 1973), pp. 24–25

[David Ketterer is a professor of English at Concordia University (Sir George Williams Campus) in Montreal, Canada. He has written extensively on genre fiction, including *New Worlds for Old* (1974), *The Rationale of Deception in Poe* (1979), and *Canadian Science Fiction and Fantasy* (1992). In this extract from his book on *Frankenstein,* Ketterer studies the notion of the Other as embodied in the monster.]

What is confusing and open-ended in *Frankenstein* results from an inability to be confident about these divisions. They constantly appear to overlap and obliterate one another. If Frankenstein's search for "the secrets of heaven and earth" is to be successful, he must be certain that he has established the limits of the Self. This is why, in searching for the secret of life and creating an artificial being, he needs to tap the *spiritual* power of electricity. Actually it might equally be argued that what Frankenstein is most fascinated by and most desires for himself is death since death is assumed to be the immediate prelude to eternal spiritual life—hence Frankenstein's efforts to create life involve much time spent in the charnel house. Nevertheless, because life is identified with a spiritual power, it follows that the creation of life does demonstrate the existence of a trancendental Other. The existence of a transcendental reality represents the ultimate hope of something beyond the Self. In *Melincourt,* Thomas Love Peacock, a friend of both the Shelleys, defines transcendentalism as the "discovery of the difference between *objective* and *subjective reality.*" Certainly, all other manifestations of the Other in *Frankenstein* are radically questioned. The people whom one "loves" may exist only as projections of the self. If the monster is actually another projection, Frankenstein's doppelgänger, then it is Frankenstein himself who murders William, Clerval and Elizabeth. But equally, both murderer and victims, together with the external universe, may be aspects of Frankenstein's mind, or Walton's mind. The possible permutations are endless.

The intermediate plasticity of reality is shown to be at one with the intermediate ontological status of the monster.

Likewise the configuration of elements that coalesced in Mary's head to produce her monstrous creation *Frankenstein* is an indeterminate mix or nexus of the "external" and "internal." This in-between state, as indicated in Chapter 4, well describes the mechanics of metaphor and it is itself the matrix of metaphor. Thus, the book, the monster and human reality are metaphors of one another. This identity owes something to the extent that all metaphor involves the confusion of the human and the non-human; a metaphoric condition is inherently monstrous.

It must be admitted that the ontology implied by the concluding paragraph of *Frankenstein* is not particularly encouraging. The sense of aloneness is overwhelming and solitude is a necessary adjunct of solipsism. The "blackness" and "distance" which surrounds and engulfs the monster (which may be taken as surrounding and engulfing human reality) looks suspiciously like a void, Locke's *tabula rasa* not externalized but actual. The transcendent in *Frankenstein* is suspiciously allied with the relationship between natural phenomena and human cognition. If the sublime experience is to be explained in terms of the mechanism of sublimation, then the possibility must be faced that what is assumed to be a transcendental Otherness may be, like all other aspects of reality, an anthropomorphic projection. But this is in no way to deny the "reality" of what comes across to every reader of Mary Shelley's novel: the "fact" that a man named Frankenstein, having discovered the secret of life and death, *does* succeed in creating a living being.

—David Ketterer, *Frankenstein's Creation: The Book, the Monster, and Human Reality* (Victoria, BC: English Literary Studies/University of Victoria, 1979), pp. 105–6

GEORGE LEVINE ON REALISM AND IMAGINATION IN
FRANKENSTEIN

[George Levine (b. 1931) is Kenneth Burke Professor of English at Rutgers University. He is the author of *The*

Boundaries of Fiction (1968) and *Darwin and the Novelists* (1988) and coeditor of *The Endurance of Frankenstein* (1979). In this extract, Levine shows how Victor Frankenstein's realization of his dream, through science, fulfills society's fears of the unbridled imagination.]

Nineteenth-century realistic fiction tends to be concerned with the possibility of accommodation to established power, and yet, given its inevitable interest in character, it explores with at least equal intensity the possibility of resistance as well. The "madwoman in the attic," to use ⟨Sandra M.⟩ Gilbert and ⟨Susan⟩ Gubar's phrase, has her male counterpart; the domesticated man—Pip, Pendennis, or Edward Waverley—has his dangerously rebellious double. Female resistance to the patriarch is echoed in a general Victorian resistance to the tyranny of society, of convention, of the majority.

Mary Shelley's characters, the monster and his creator, reflect the culture's ambivalence about itself, the realist's difficulty with the narrative conventions of realism. As creator, Frankenstein attempts to reach beyond the limits of human possibility, as the realists reached beyond words, into reality. Yet when he finds what his imagination has brought forth, he recoils from it as monstrous, and denies kinship. Thus denied, the monster in effect destroys all that belongs to a recognizably domestic world: the child, the caring friend, the affectionate servant, the all-providing father (whose death he only indirectly causes) and, most important, the bride on her wedding night. The consummation of community, the confirmation of a justly ordered world, the affirmation of consonance between word and action, the marriage turns out to be a murder. All the potential horrors of domestic realism, so carefully averted in the comic tradition, are anticipated here.

The attempt to repress and then destroy the monster leads Frankenstein and his book into a landscape beyond the limits of the domestic realism toward which they had turned for succor. Such landscapes provide the spaces, distant from the centers of realistic drama, in which illicit and uncivilized extremes are acted out. The assumption of most nineteenth-century literature, from Scott forward, is that civilization was indeed advancing. The Macaulayan reading of history implied that savagery had been banished from the centers of Western experience. But in *Frankenstein,* Alps and Arctic wastes are the norm. They are the landscape of isolation from community, Victor's first obsessive choice, and they are the icons of his refusal to bring the monster in from the cold to the communal warmth of the hearth. In the cold, monster and creator enact the futility of their desires in what is almost a ritual and self-destructive parody of the Keatsian quest for the elusive fair maiden. Only Captain Walton returns, and only because he surrenders his Frankensteinian ambition. In its place, he finds an ear for the narrative in his sister, the civilized Mrs. Saville. Telling the story is made possible by the refusal to live it, and is a means to rejoin the community. His position is rather like Mary Shelley's, for she surrenders fully to her imagination, but in the writing she keeps the distance that might save her from it and deny it.

The parabolic neatness of this way of telling the story (certainly a distortion of the novel's instability and ambiguities) suggests why, for the past one hundred sixty years, it has provided metaphors for writers. The monster becomes those sexual, revolutionary, deterministic, or psychic energies that novelists and intellectuals confront even as they try to avert them. It is both rational and irrational, victim and victimizer, innocent and evil. As in the culture at large, Frankenstein and his monster keep turning up in literature—in the face of the uneducated mob in *Mary Barton,* in Magwitch's relation to Pip, his created gentleman, in the laboratories where Ursula Brangwen studies. The power of the myth of *Frankenstein* transcends the limit of the particular narrative because it is, in a way, an antimyth that has embodied in all its ambiguities the modern imagination of the potentialities and the limits of modern consciousness. ⟨. . .⟩

Moreover, *Frankenstein*'s preoccupation with "creation"—though connected with literary myths and Mary Shelley's own concern with birth—is more than accidentally related to the problems and responsibilities of writing itself. Mary Shelley obviously belongs in the Romantic tradition of concern about the nature of creativity, about the relation of mind to nature, of mind to itself, and about the possibility that language—particularly poetic language—might live actively in the real world. Belonging to a literature of extremes, *Frankenstein* is nevertheless an act of rebellion against those extremes. It dramatizes, whatever its intentions, the deadliness of Shelley, her husband's, idealizing and rebellion, the consequences of Godwin, her father's, personal tyranny and his antithetic radicalism, the perversion in myths of male creativity and female dependence. In this respect, it is analogous to realism's parodic reaction to romance and to fantasies of extreme power. Like the protagonists to be disenchanted in later novels, Walton, Frankenstein, and the monster all find some radical disparity between what they read and what they experience. Each character must face the consequences of that disparity and come to terms with the limits of dream, yet the text itself is—like much realism—paradoxically Promethean. The realist novel rejects earlier fantasies of power for the limits of the probable, hoping to touch the real.

—George Levine, *The Realistic Imagination: English Fiction from* Frankenstein *to* Lady Chatterley (Chicago: University of Chicago Press, 1981), pp. 24–26

BARBARA JOHNSON ON FRANKENSTEIN'S MONSTER AS A SYMBOL FOR THE FEAR OF CHILDBIRTH

[Barbara Johnson (b. 1947), a professor of French and comparative literature at Yale University, is the author of *The Critical Difference: Essays in the Contemporary Rhetoric of Reading* (1981), *A World of Difference* (1987), *The Consequences of Theory* (1990), and other works utilizing poststructuralist critical theories. In this extract, Johnson analyzes *Frankenstein* as exemplifying the fear of childbirth and probes the possible autobiographical sources for this fear.]

It is only recently that critics have begun to see Victor Frankenstein's disgust at the sight of his creation as a study of postpartum depression, as a representation of maternal rejection of a newborn infant, and to relate the entire novel to Mary Shelley's mixed feelings about motherhood. Having lived through an unwanted pregnancy from a man married to someone else only to see that baby die, followed by a second baby named William—which is the name of the Monster's first murder victim—Mary Shelley, at the age of only eighteen, must have had excruciatingly divided emotions. Her own mother, indeed, had died upon giving her birth. The idea that a mother can loathe, fear, and reject her baby has until recently been one of the most repressed of psychoanalytical insights, although it is of course already implicit in the story of Oedipus, whose parents cast him out as an infant to die. What is threatening about each of these books is the way in which its critique of the *role* of the mother touches on primitive terrors of the mother's rejection of the child. Each of these women writers *does* in her way reject the child as part of her coming to grips with the untenable nature of mother love: Nancy Friday decides not to have children, Dorothy Dinnerstein argues that men as well as women should do the mothering, and Mary Shelley describes a parent who flees in disgust from the repulsive being to whom he has just given birth.

Yet it is not merely in its depiction of the ambivalence of motherhood that Mary Shelley's novel can be read as autobiographical. In the introductory note added in 1831, she writes:

> The publishers of the standard novels, in selecting *Frankenstein* for one of their series, expressed a wish that I should furnish them with some account of the origin of the story. I am the more willing to comply because I shall thus give a general answer to the question so very frequently asked me—how I, then a young girl, came to think of and to *dilate upon* so very hideous an idea. *[emphasis mine]*

As this passage makes clear, readers of Mary Shelley's novel had frequently expressed the feeling that a young girl's fascination with the idea of monstrousness was somehow monstrous in itself. When Mary ends her introduction to the re-edition of her novel with the words: "And now, once again, I bid my hideous progeny go forth and prosper," the reader begins to suspect that there may perhaps be meaningful parallels between Victor's creation of his monster and Mary's creation of her book.

Such parallels are indeed unexpectedly pervasive. The impulse to write the book and the desire to search for the secrets of animation both arise under the same seemingly trivial circumstances: the necessity of finding something to read on a rainy day. During inclement weather on a family vacation, Victor Frankenstein happens upon the writings of Cornelius Agrippa, and is immediately fired with the longing to penetrate the secrets of life and death. Similarly, it was during a wet, ungenial summer in Switzerland that Mary, Shelley, Byron, and several others picked up a volume of ghost stories and decided to write a collection of spine-tingling tales of their own. Moreover, Mary's discovery of the subject she would write about is described in almost exactly the same words as Frankenstein's discovery of the principle of life: "Swift as light and as cheering was the idea that broke in upon me," writes Mary in her introduction, while Frankenstein says: "From the midst of this darkness a sudden light broke in upon me." In both cases the sudden flash of inspiration must be supported by the meticulous gathering of heterogeneous, ready-made materials: Frankenstein collects bones and organs; Mary records overheard discussions of scientific questions that lead her to her sudden vision of monstrous creation. "Invention," she writes of the process of writing, but her words apply equally well to Frankenstein's labors, "Invention . . . does not consist in creating out of the void, but out of chaos; the materials must, in the first place, be afforded: it can give form to dark, shapeless substances but cannot bring into being the substance itself." Perhaps the most revealing indication of Mary's identification of Frankenstein's activity with her own is to be found in her use of the word "artist" on two different occasions to qualify the "pale student of unhallowed arts": "His success would terrify the *artist*," she writes of the catastrophic moment of creation, while Frankenstein confesses to Walton: "I appeared rather like one doomed by slavery to toil in the mines, or any other unwholesome trade than an *artist* occupied by his favorite employment."

—Barbara Johnson, "My Monster/My Self," *Diacritics* 12, No. 2 (Summer 1982): 6–7

[Paul A. Cantor (b. 1945) is a professor of English at the University of Virginia and a noted Shakespeare scholar, having written *Shakespeare's Rome: Republic and Empire* (1976) and *Shakespeare:* Hamlet (1989). In this extract, Cantor argues that Victor Frankenstein's childhood aggression corrupted his later scientific passions, resulting in the creation of the monster.]

Given the link between creator and creature in *Frankenstein,* discussions of Frankenstein as a character and of the monster as a character tend to shade into each other, that is, one can approach either character through analyzing the other. In studying Frankenstein, one readily sees how the monster can be regarded as an extension of his creator, in a sense as a projection of Frankenstein's psyche. The more difficult task is to show in analyzing the monster's character how in a strange sense Frankenstein can be regarded as a projection of the creature's psyche.

The key to understanding Frankenstein's character can be found in the detailed portrait of his childhood Mary Shelley creates. Victor himself sees a connection between his idealistic pursuit of science and his childhood aggressiveness: "My temper was sometimes violent, and my passions vehement; but by some law in my temperature they were turned not towards childish pursuits but to an eager desire to learn." Given the eventual results of Frankenstein's experiments, we should not be surprised to hear that his interest in science was originally a sublimation of his violent impulses. But the most important fact we learn about Frankenstein's youth is his attitude toward Elizabeth, the little orphan girl his family takes in. Here Mary Shelley introduces a displaced incest motif, a familiar device in Romantic fiction. Victor calls Elizabeth his "more than sister," and indeed their relationship has all the potential for incest except the blood tie. They grow up in the same household, share the same childhood experiences, and have a secret bond of sympathy, much as do Catherine and Heathcliff in *Wuthering Heights.* Even when presented in displaced form, an incestuous relationship involves an inward-turning of energies, a refusal to leave the self-contained world of childhood desires and dreams, that is the central impulse in Frankenstein's life.

—Paul A. Cantor, *Creature and Creator: Myth-Making and English Romanticism* (Cambridge: Cambridge University Press, 1984), pp. 109–10, 114–15

JOYCE CAROL OATES ON DIDACTICISM IN *FRANKENSTEIN*

[Joyce Carol Oates (b. 1938) is one of the most important contemporary novelists; among her many works are several modern Gothic novels, including *A Bloodsmoor Romance* (1982) and *Mysteries of Winterthurn* (1984). She is currently Roger S. Berlind Distinguished Professor at Princeton University. In this extract, Oates asserts that *Frankenstein* is a didactic novel and a forerunner of science fiction in its depiction of a world without God.]

⟨. . .⟩ it is a mistake to read *Frankenstein* as a modern novel of psychological realism, or as a "novel" at all. It contains no characters, only points of view; its concerns are pointedly moral and didactic; it makes no claims for verisimilitude of even a poetic Wordsworthian nature. (The Alpine landscapes are all self-consciously sublime and theatrical; Mont Blanc, for instance, suggests "another earth, the habitations of another race of beings.") If one were to choose a literary antecedent for *Frankenstein* it might be, surprisingly, Samuel Johnson's *Rasselas,* rather than a popular Gothic like Mrs. Radcliffe's *Mysteries of Udolpho,* which allegedly had the power to frighten its readers. (A character in Jane Austen's *Northanger Abbey* says of this once famous novel: "I remember finishing it in two days—my hair standing on end the whole time.") Though *Frankenstein* and *Dracula* are commonly linked, Bram Stoker's tour-de-force of 1897 is vastly different in tone, theme, and intention from Shelley's novel: its "monster" is not at all monstrous in appearance, only in behavior; and he is thoroughly and irremediably evil by nature. But no one in *Frankenstein* is evil—the universe is emptied of God and theistic assumptions of "good" and "evil." Hence its modernity.

Tragedy does not arise spontaneous and unwilled in so "modern" a setting, it must be made—in fact, manufactured. The Fates are not to blame; there *are* no Fates; only the brash young scientist who boasts of never having feared the supernatural. ("In my education my father had taken the greatest precautions that my mind should be impressed with no supernatural horrors. I do not ever remember to have trembled at a tale of superstition, or to have feared the apparition of a spirit. . . . A churchyard was to me merely the receptacle of bodies deprived of life, which, from being the seat of beauty and strength, had become food for the worm.") Where *Dracula* and other conventional Gothic works are fantasies, with clear links to fairly tales and legends, and even popular ballads, *Frankenstein* has the theoretical and cautionary tone of science fiction. It is meant to prophecize, not to entertain.

—Joyce Carol Oates, "Afterword: Frankenstein's Fallen Angel," *Frankenstein; or, The Modern Prometheus* by Mary Shelley (West Hatfield, CT: Pennyroyal Press, 1984), pp. 248–49

MARGARET HOMANS ON THE SUBVERSION OF MOTHERHOOD

[Margaret Homans (b. 1952) is a professor of English at Yale University and a prominent feminist critic. Among her works are *Women Writers and Poetic Identity* (1980) and *Bearing the Word: Language and Female Experience in Nineteenth-Century Woman's Writing* (1986), from which the following extract is taken. Here, Homans points out the frequent deaths of mothers in *Frankenstein* and relates it to Victor Frankenstein's desire to subvert the role of the mother by discovering the secrets of human creation through science.]

Many readers of *Frankenstein* have noted both that the demon's creation amounts to an elaborate circumvention of normal heterosexual procreation—Frankenstein does by himself with great difficulty what a heterosexual couple can do quite easily—and that each actual mother dies very rapidly upon being introduced as a character in the novel. Frankenstein's own history is full of the deaths of mothers. His mother was discovered, as a poverty-stricken orphan, by Frankenstein's father. Frankenstein's adoptive sister and later fiancée, Elizabeth, was likewise discovered as an orphan, in poverty, by Frankenstein's parents. Elizabeth catches scarlet fever, and her adoptive mother, nursing her, catches it herself and dies of it. On her deathbed, the mother hopes for the marriage of Elizabeth and Frankenstein and tells Elizabeth, "You must supply my place to my younger children" (chap. 3). Like Shelley herself, Elizabeth is the death of her mother and becomes a substitute for her. Justine, a young girl taken in by the Frankenstein family as a beloved servant, is said to cause the death of her mother; and Justine herself, acting as foster mother to Frankenstein's little brother, William, is executed for his murder. There are many mothers in the Frankenstein circle, and all die notable deaths.

The significance of the apparently necessary destruction of the mother first emerges in Frankenstein's account of his preparations for creating the demon, and it is confirmed soon after the demon comes to life. Of his early passion for science, Frankenstein says, "I was . . . deeply smitten with the thirst for knowledge" (chap. 2). Shelley confirms the oedipal suggestion here when she writes that it is despite his father's prohibition that the young boy devours the archaic books on natural philosophy that first raise his ambitions to discover the secret of life. His mother dies just as Frankenstein is preparing to go to the University of Ingolstadt, and if his postponed trip there is thus motivated by her death, what he finds at the university becomes a substitute for her: modern scientists, he is told, "penetrate into the recesses of nature and show how she works in her hiding-places" (chap. 3). Frankenstein's double, Walton, the polar explorer who rescues him and records his story, likewise searches for what sound like sexual secrets, also in violation of a paternal prohibition. Seeking to "satiate [his] ardent curiosity," Walton hopes to find the "wondrous power which attracts the needle" (letter 1). Frankenstein, having become "capable of bestowing animation upon lifeless matter," feels that to arrive "at once at the summit of my desires was the most gratifying consummation of my toils." And his work to create the demon adds to this sense of an oedipal violation of Mother Nature: dabbling "among the unhallowed damps of the grave," he "disturbed, with profane fingers, the tremendous secrets of the human frame" (chap. 4). This violation is necrophiliac. The mother he rapes is dead; his researches into her secrets, to usurp her powers, require that she be dead.

—Margaret Homans, "Bearing Demons: Frankenstein's Circumvention of the Maternal," *Bearing the Word: Language and Female Experience in Nineteenth-Century Woman's Writing* (Chicago: University of Chicago Press, 1986), pp. 101–2

❖

WILLIAM VEEDER ON VICTOR FRANKENSTEIN'S FEAR OF HIS WIFE

[William Veeder is a professor of English at the University of Chicago. He is the author of *Henry James: The Lessons of the Master* (1975) and the editor of Dr. Jekyll and Mr. Hyde *After One Hundred Years* (1988). In the following extract, taken from his book on Mary Shelley, Veeder argues that some parts of the novel could be interpreted as suggesting Victor Frankenstein's fear of female sexuality and, consequently, an unconscious fear of his wife Elizabeth.]

Victor's questions—"Why am I here to relate the destruction.... Could I behold this and live?"—encourage us to question many of his acts, to see the will beneath the sympathy. Why, for example, does Victor not thwart the monster beforehand, either by destroying it outright or by understanding its threat? Destroying the monster is definitely possible. "I would have seized him; but he eluded me." Victor then asks our question: "Why had I not followed him, and closed with him in mortal strife?" Our suspicion that "I suffered him to depart" because Victor did not really want him stopped is strengthened after the murder when the creature "eluded me." The repetition of "eluded me" emphasizes how little has changed in the elusive relation of creator and creature. The monster escapes both times because he effects what Victor wants each time. This is also why Victor fails to understand the monster's threat. " '*I will be with you on your wedding night!*' Such was my sentence." The sentence against Victor as bridegroom is pronounced by Victor as monster. The actual meaning of the threat becomes clear to Frankenstein too late, just as Elizabeth is embraced by him on the marriage bed too late. "I will kill thee, / And love thee after," says Othello, speaking for the sons of Eros (5.2.18–19). Only after the fact can Frankenstein do what he should have done earlier, because only now is the failure assured which is Victor-y.

The monster's threat indicates how Mary Shelley uses formal elements to reveal Victor's murderous will on the wedding night. As the threat is open to two interpretations, and as Victor is operating on both conscious and unconscious levels, she provides a second, subversive layer to language also. "[I resolved] not to join her until I had obtained some knowledge as to the situation of my ememy. She . . ." By "enemy" Victor consciously means the monster, of course. But "my enemy. She" suggests that the real enemy is Elizabeth. A similar use of language has occurred a few lines earlier: "I resolved . . . not [to] relax the impending conflict until my own life, or that of my adversary, were extinguished. Elizabeth . . ." The words "my adversary were extinguished. Elizabeth" say more than Victor consciously intends. "Extinguished Elizabeth" is what will allow him to relax. That "my adversary" can be "Elizabeth" is emphasized by Victor's first calling their honeymoon house a "retreat" and then vowing to inspect "every corner that might afford a retreat to my adversary." In this battle of the sexes, Victor "reflected how dreadful the combat . . . would be to my wife." He means literally that Elizabeth would be frightened by his battling a monster, but unconsciously he knows how much more dreadful will be her own battle with the monster. That battle ends with Elizabeth's "dreadful" scream.

—William Veeder, *Mary Shelley and* Frankenstein: *The Fate of Androgyny* (Chicago: University of Chicago Press, 1986), pp. 119–20

[Chris Baldick (b. 1954) is Lecturer in English at Edge
Hill College of Higher Education in Omskirk, England,
and the author of *The Social Mission of English
Criticism 1848–1932* (1983) and *In Frankenstein's
Shadow* (1987), from which the following excerpt is
taken. Here, Baldick maintains that *Frankenstein* is
chiefly a rumination on the double-edged nature of
knowledge, which can lead both to great benefits and
great disasters for humanity.]

Rather than tie *Frankenstein* too soon to the issue of technology
as such, it would be safer to say that the novel dramatizes certain doubts about the rewards of knowledge, in a broader
sense. Knowledge is shown to be double-edged, its benefits
and hazards depending upon the circumstances, and the spirit,
in which it is pursued. It is not just Victor's experience which
shows this; in many ways the monster learns the lesson more
clearly. Mary Shelley's description of his first experiences is
designed as an accelerated expostion both of infant development and of the early history of the human species. This
empiricist version of Adam's story is perhaps partly inspired by
Volney's *Ruins*, a book from which the monster learns of
human history, and in which the chapter on the 'Original State
of Men' presents the earliest man as 'an orphan, deserted by
the unknown power that had produced him', learning purely
by his senses. A crucial stage in the monster's education comes
with his discovery of fire:

> One day, when I was oppressed by cold, I found a fire which
> had been left by some wandering beggars, and was overcome
> with delight at the warmth I experienced from it. In my joy I
> thrust my hand into the live embers, but quickly drew it out
> again with a cry of pain. How strange, I thought, that the same
> cause should produce such opposite effects!

In discovering pain and pleasure arising from the same
source, the monster has felt the contradictory nature of experience. He will feel its confusing force again in the 'mixture of
pain and pleasure' inspired in him by the De Laceys' affections
and in the record of human history which displays us as both

vicious and virtuous. His empiricist translation of the Eden and Prometheus myths here obviously preserves their sense of the ambivalence of knowledge, and in this episode at least it is the monster rather than Victor who is the modern Prometheus. Unlike Victor but like Prometheus, he uses his knowledge helpfully, collecting firewood for the De Laceys; but it is with fire too that he destroys their cottage and later himself.

The monster's further reflections on his discoveries also condense the novel's issues. As he compares his own position (and his appearance) with that of the De Laceys, he finds that 'sorrow only increase[s] with knowledge'. 'Increase of knowledge', he adds later, 'only discovered to me more clearly what a wretched outcast I was.' This is another lesson which Victor too—like Godwin's heroes—has to learn more slowly and painfully: the condition of solitude cannot be cured, only sharpened, by knowledge. All three of the narrators in the novel are self-educated, and fall victim to this problem; seeking knowledge *in* solitude, they are condemned to find only a more distressing knowledge *of* solitude. Bearing in mind this implied critique of solitude—to which we shall need to return later—we can concede that the novel is indeed about the perils of discovery.

A straightforward cautionary tale, however, it is not. Although Mary Shelley's revisions and Introduction of 1831 did, as we shall see, nudge the story in the direction of a parable of presumption, the grounds for this sort of reading are shifting and uncertain in the text as a whole, particularly in the first edition of 1818. The novel's inconclusiveness breaks out at the very moment when Victor Frankenstein seems to be drawing most tidily the moral of the tale:

> Farewell, Walton! Seek happiness in tranquility, and avoid ambition, even if it be only the apparently innocent one of distinguishing yourself in science and discoveries. Yet why do I say this? I have myself been blasted in these hopes, yet another may succeed.

This last escape clause could be read as evidence of Victor's incorrigible blindness, but it seems more likely to be an equivocation of Mary Shelley's own, perhaps reflecting her mixed feelings about her literary ambitions, and apparently aligning her with her mother's refusal to endorse the superstitions of Pandora's box and similar anti-scientific fables. In this sense *Frankenstein* shares in that duplicity with which many Gothic novels (*Vathek, The Monk,* and *Zastrozzi* among them) appear to reprove their villains while covertly driving them on to futher blasphemous outrages. At the eleventh hour the text defers judgement, allowing true progress and discovery still to be made by 'another'—by those who find a way out of the trap in which Frankenstein has been caught.

—Chris Baldick, *In Frankenstein's Shadow: Myth, Monstrosity, and Nineteenth-Century Writing* (Oxford: Clarendon Press, 1987), pp. 45–47

Stephen C. Behrendt on Mary Shelley's Use of Language

[Stephen C. Behrendt (b. 1947) is the author of *The Moment of Explosion: Blake and the Illustration of Milton* (1983), *Shelley and His Audience* (1989), and *History and Myth: Essays on English Romantic Literature* (1990). He is a professor of English at the University of Nebraska. In this extract, Behrendt illustrates how Victor Frankenstein's feeble attempts to destroy the monster are reflected by the passive sentence constructions he utters.]

When Victor does finally engage the Creature in an active-voice interchange, as on the Mer de Glace, it is to threaten and to condemn, not to establish community: "There can be no community between you and me; we are enemies." Elsewhere, he relegates to dependent clauses his acts and activities whose consequences are the greatest and most terrible. Other illustrations of Victor's preference for passive construction abound, particularly those linked with long and elaborate sentence structures. In tracing them, students come to appreciate how much this man of words isolates and insulates himself in a fabric of deception whose raw material is language itself.

This language-bound novel returns again and again to crucial events that depend on successful or, more commonly, failed or suppressed communication. As her father does in *Caleb Williams*, Mary Shelley explores in *Frankenstein* the consequences of repressing communication. Godwin's Caleb fears that the "truth" he knows about Falkland is too fabulous to be believed (and in both the endings Godwin composed Caleb suffers a mental collapse); similarly, Victor believes that what he knows about the murder of William, for which Justine pays the price, would be regarded as "the ravings of insanity." Consequently, he resolves "to remain silent," even as he consistently refuses to tell Clerval or anyone else what he has been doing. The unnatural quality of such suppression is underscored by Victor's increasingly hysterical behavior and by the apparent disease (of a clearly psychological origin) to which he falls victim after the Creature escapes from the laboratory. Significantly, once his "illness" passes, he resumes his correspondence with Elizabeth.

Still, Victor Frankenstein "remain[s] silent" almost to the end. Only on board Walton's ice-bound vessel does he at last find the friend and confessor to whom he can pour out his tale, much as the Ancient Mariner's prayer springs forth when he recognizes the dignity of life and blesses the water snakes. Only at the end of his life, once he has presented his history as a monologue, does Victor engage at last in the apparently unprejudiced and noncompetitive conversation to which he had been a stranger since his youth. Walton's comment is important: "His eloquence is forcible and touching; nor can I hear him, when he relates a pathetic incident or endeavours to move the passions of pity or love, without tears." At the terrible cost of his own life and those of family and friends, Victor finally learns to communicate. Yet even this effort is not entirely guileless egalitarian communication. Victor is still attempting, from his deathbed, to control events by means of words, exerting psychological pressure where physical force is no longer possible. His speech to Walton's unwilling sailors offers clear evidence of his recalcitrance, as does his dying request that Walton "undertake [his] unfinished work" and destroy the Creature. Who can refuse a dying person's last request? Walton can, we discover, and his expression of that refusal (and the soul-searching it entails) to his sister—who represents the warmth, family, and community toward which he has now redirected his ship and his thoughts—is a gesture of courage and self-sufficiency.

—Stephen C. Behrendt, "Language and Style in *Frankenstein*," *Approaches to Teaching Shelley's* Frankenstein, ed. Stephen C. Behrendt (New York: Modern Language Association of America, 1990), pp. 82–83

❖

Diana Basham on Victor Frankenstein and a Female Monster

[Diana Basham is the author of *The Trial of Women: Feminism and the Occult Sciences in Victorian Literature and Society* (1992), from which the following extract is taken. Here, Basham maintains that Victor Frankenstein's refusal to create a female mate for the monster suggests his fear of a "superwoman" who might be uncontrollable by men.]

It is perhaps no exaggeration to say that Victorian feminism began to develop in conjunction with the occult the moment when Victor Frankenstein decided not to create a female companion for his sinister scientific monster. The task of doing so descended unfulfilled to the next generation of novelists and was taken up by Victorian writers concerned to shape the 'New Woman' who would stand as emblem for their period's variously constructed achievements. Sitting in his moonlit laboratory, Mary Shelley's harassed scientist reconsiders the promise he has made to his half-human creation and decides that, abhorrent as the monster itself is, a female variant might be 'ten thousand times more malignant than her mate and delight, for its own sake, in murder and wretchedness'. Frankenstein fears that a female monster 'might refuse to comply with a compact made before her creation', and that, as the superwoman of a new race, the old Eve might re-assert her lawless ways and endanger the future of the human species. 'Had I the right', he asks himself, 'to inflict this curse upon everlasting generations?' Frankenstein destroys 'the half finished creature', puts the relics in a basket and drops them into the sea, whence, like other creatures of the Victorian imagination, they would re-emerge assembled in the likeness of Rider Haggard's Ayesha in *She,* or Bulwer Lytton's Zee in *The Coming Race.* An early version of Jack the Ripper, mutilating female corpses in order to be free of the dangerous womb, Frankenstein's scientific project is everywhere related to his preoccupation with motherhood and his ambivalent wish to remove the 'curse' with which it is associated.

The trouble begins for Frankenstein with the onset of puberty. The idyll of his childhood is interrupted when he himself disobeys his father's injunction and begins to study the occult science of alchemy. As the terminology of the alchemists is deeply reliant upon menstrual analogies, it is symbolically appropriate that Frankenstein's sixteen-year-old adoptive sister, Elizabeth, whose female nature he regards as quite literally 'a possession of my own', suddenly develops an attack of 'Scarlet fever', which causes the death of Frankenstein's mother. The death of the mother is a significant event in Frankenstein's career. It simultaneously confirms his determination to gain control over 'the principle of life' without the intervening female medium and at the same time puts him in contact with the means by which he can do it. Frankenstein's alchemic obsessions are associated with his mother; it is only after her death that he is able to transfer his enthusiasms to a modern chemistry which had previously 'seemed to limit itself to the annihilation of those visions on which my interest in science was chiefly founded.'

—Diana Basham, *The Trial of Women: Feminism and the Occult Sciences in Victorian Literature and Society* (New York: New York University Press, 1992), pp. 5–6

[David Soyka has done graduate work at Rutgers University (Newark Campus). In this extract, Soyka ponders the relationship between Mary Shelley's novel and Milton's *Paradise Lost,* especially in the possible parallel between God and Frankenstein on the one hand and Satan and the monster on the other.]

The modern Prometheus, then, is the unthinking creator who fails, whether intentionally or unconsciously, to be responsible for his creation, thereby creating evil. But the responsibilities of creation go beyond issues related to modern science and technology, or even, to accept another reading of the novel, modern man's psychological conflicts. The underlying theme is rooted in Miltonic questions about the first creation. If God is the creator of all things, why did He create evil to ruin his creation? And if, despite being the prime source of all things, the creator is somehow excused from creating evil, why does He continue to allow evil to be inflicted upon His creation? Does God truly play dice with the universe? And if he does, is He totally shed of any responsibility when the dice come up "snake eyes"? Certainly Victor Frankenstein plays a poor game of dice. An examination of Shelley's portrayal of Victor's character and motivations reveals her thoughts about this Miltonic dilemma. ⟨. . .⟩

Shelley suggests we and not our stars are to blame, but without quite letting God off the hook. It strikes us as incomprehensible that Frankenstein so readily abandons his creation after entertaining fantasies that a "new species would bless me as its creator and source; many happy and excellent natures would owe their being to me. No father should claim the gratitude of his child so completely as I should deserve theirs." We might at first think of Adam and Eve's banishment from the Garden of Eden in Genesis 3, but this doesn't quite fit since God does not entirely abandon humanity to its own devices, as Frankenstein does the Monster. The analogy here is not to the Bible but to Milton's *Paradise Lost* depiction of God as disappointed in His creation of Satan. Instead of admonishing Satan, or somehow metaphysically remedying Satan's inclination towards pride, God casts Satan out forever from His domain. Similarly, Frankenstein's disappointment in his creation causes him to cast out the Monster, who he continually refers to thereafter as "fiend" or "devil." One reason why the reader can sympathize with Frankenstein's Monster as well as with Milton's Satan is that despite whatever evil they cause, they have been abandoned, seemingly without substantial cause, by their respective creators. In both cases, we have to ask, without necessarily receiving a satisfactory answer, how these two expulsions can possibly take place without any consideration of what further complications may be caused. And, in both cases, the cast-out doesn't take his revenge directly upon the Creator, the cause of his predicament, but upon the innocent beings important to the Creator (Adam and Eve; Victor's close friend and relations).

Why an Omniscient Being would purposely create circumstances to create evil, but in such a way to allow apologists such as Milton to provide excuses for providential behavior, is a theological question that readers of Milton and apologists for Christianity argued over at least up to Shelley's time. That Victor Frankenstein, a rational man of science, would be so unthinking is not really as inexplicable. Even just up to Mary Shelley's time, the pages of history are more than filled with the follies of supposedly rational men. As Mellor points out, "Writing during the early years of Britain's industrial revolution and the age of Empire, Mary Shelley was aware of the damaging consequences of a scientific, objective, alienated view of both nature and human labor." Moreover, as Donald M. Hassler observes, "The end of the eighteenth century also witnessed the diabolical transformation of progress into the terror of French Revolution."

—David Soyka, "Frankenstein and the Miltonic Creation of Evil," Extrapolation 33, No. 2 (Summer 1992): 167–68, 170–71

[Katherine C. Hill-Miller is the author of *"My Hideous
Progeny"* (1995), a book studying Mary Shelley's relation to her father, William Godwin. In the following
extract from this book, Hill-Miller believes that society's rejection of Frankenstein's monster can be read in
part as a reflection of Mary Shelley's own sense of
rejection by her father.]

If Frankenstein's creature can be read as an embodiment of the
female, it can also be read more specifically as representing
the plight of the daughter. Shelley takes pains to underscore
the similarities between the situation of the creature and the
predicament of the other abandoned, rejected, or betrayed
daughters with whom she populates the pages of *Frankenstein.*
Although Frankenstein's nameless creature is emphatically
male, his circumstances have much more in common with the
daughters who appear in the novel than with the sons. Chief
among the similarities is the fact that the creature is "an orphan
and beggar"—a condition to which, at some point in the novel,
all the daughters in *Frankenstein* have been reduced by their
fathers. On the opening page of Frankenstein's narration,
Shelley presents the story of Caroline Beaufort, Frankenstein's
mother. Caroline Beaufort was motherless; she was cast into
helpless poverty when her father lost his fortune and died.
Society did not allow her the means to support herself; she was
saved from penury and wretchedness only because Alphonse
Frankenstein found her and allowed her to depend on him for
protection. Similarly, Elizabeth Lavenza, Frankenstein's cousin,
was sent from her family home when her mother died and her
father remarried. She was saved because Alphonse
Frankenstein, her kindly uncle, was willing to take her into his
house. Justine Moritz, a Frankenstein family servant who is
eventually accused of murdering Victor Frankenstein's younger
brother, is made into "an orphan and beggar" when first her
father dies and then her mother. Shelley further emphasizes the
connection between Justine and Frankenstein's creature when
Justine, explaining why she succumbed to her confessor's pressure to admit to a crime she did not commit, exclaims, "I

almost began to think that I was the monster that he said I was." Even Safie, the Arabian girl who falls in love with Felix DeLacey at the center of the creature's narration, is orphaned of a mother and betrayed by her father. The histories of these daughters all serve to suggest Shelley's recognition of the pitifully dependent circumstances to which female children can be brought by the absence of a mother and the abandonment of a father. But they also point to and parallel the plight of the novel's central character. Like these daughters, Frankenstein's creature is motherless, has been abandoned by his father, and has thus been reduced to the condition of "an orphan and a beggar." The difference is that the other daughters in *Frankenstein* find some haven of male protection and are thus not driven to rebellion and revenge. For Frankenstein's offspring, devoid of any social ties or saving human affection, the story is very different.

Some details of the creature's early history link him to a very specific daughter: Mary Shelley herself. As the creature hides in the hovel behind the DeLacey cottage, he reads *Paradise Lost,* a volume of Plutarch's *Lives,* and the *Sorrows of Werter*—all works that Mary Shelley read as she prepared to write *Frankenstein.* Motherless and rejected by her own father as she wrote *Frankenstein,* Mary Shelley gives the creature her own obsessive fascination with her "accursed origin" (126). Most important, Mary Shelley uses Frankenstein's rejected offspring to express her own rage and aggression, in particular at William Godwin and in general at cultural fathers whose power and prerogatives rob daughters of autonomy by associating them with sexuality, filth, and death. As U. C. Knoepflmacher has persuasively argued, *Frankenstein* is to a large degree a revenge tale in which Frankenstein's creature punishes his neglectful father/creator by forcing him to experience the creature's own desolation. The centrality of rage and revenge to the meaning of *Frankenstein* explain Shelley's decision to cast the figure of the betrayed daughter as a male: in the guise of a gigantic male, Frankenstein's offspring possesses vast power, specifically the physical power to avenge itself through murder.

—Katherine C. Hill-Miller, *"My Hideous Progeny": Mary Shelley, William Godwin, and the Father-Daughter Relationship* (Newark: University of Delaware Press, 1995), pp. 67–68

❧

Books by
Mary Shelley

History of a Six Weeks' Tour through a Part of France, Switzerland, Germany and Holland (with Percy Bysshe Shelley). 1817.

Frankenstein; or, The Modern Prometheus. 1818. 3 vols.

Valperga; or, The Life and Adventures of Castruccio, Prince of Lucca. 1823. 3 vols.

Posthumous Poems by Percy Bysshe Shelley (editor). 1824.

The Last Man. 1826. 3 vols.

The Fortunes of Perkin Warbeck: A Romance. 1830. 3 vols.

Lodore. 1835. 3 vols.

Falkner. 1837. 3 vols.

Poetical Works by Percy Bysshe Shelley (editor). 1839. 4 vols.

Essays, Letters from Abroad, Translations and Fragments by Percy Bysshe Shelley (editor). 1840. 2 vols.

Rambles in Germany and Italy in 1840, 1842, and 1843. 1844. 2 vols.

The Choice: A Poem on Shelley's Death. Ed. H. Buxton Forman. 1876.

Tales and Stories. Ed. Richard Garnett. 1891.

Letters, Mostly Unpublished. Ed. Henry H. Harper. 1918.

Proserpine and Midas: Mythological Dramas. Ed. André Henri Koszul. 1922.

Harriet and Mary: Being the Relations between P. B., Harriet and Mary Shelley and T. J. Hogg as Shown in Letters between Them (with others). Ed. Walter Sidney Scott. 1944.

Letters. Ed. Frederick L. Jones. 1944. 2 vols.

Journal. Ed. Frederick L. Jones. 1947.

My Best Mary: Selected Letters. Ed. Muriel Spark and Derek Stanford. 1953.

Matilda. Ed. Elizabeth Nitchie. 1959.

Shelley's Posthumous Poems: Mary Shelley's Fair Copy Book (editor). Ed. Irving Massey. 1969.

Collected Tales and Stories. Ed. Charles E. Robinson. 1976.

Letters. Ed. Betty T. Bennett. 1980–88. 3 vols.

Journals. Ed. Paula R. Feldman and Diana Scott-Kilvert. 1987. 2 vols.

The Mary Shelley Reader. Ed. Betty T. Bennett and Charles E. Robinson. 1990.

Works about Mary Shelley and Frankenstein

Bloom, Harold, ed. *Mary Shelley.* New York: Chelsea House, 1985.

———, ed. *Mary Shelley's* Frankenstein. New York: Chelsea House, 1987.

Blumberg, Jane. *Mary Shelley's Early Novels: This Child of Imagination and Misery.* Iowa City: University of Iowa Press, 1993.

Botting, Fred. *Making Monstrous:* Frankenstein, *Criticism, Theory.* Manchester, UK: Manchester University Press, 1991.

Brennan, Matthew C. "The Landscape of Grief in Mary Shelley's *Frankenstein.*" *Studies in the Humanities* 15 (1988): 33–44.

Carson, James P. "Bringing the Author Forward: *Frankenstein* through Mary Shelley's Letters." *Criticism* 30 (1988): 431–53.

Clubbe, John. "The Tempest-Toss'd Summer of 1816: Mary Shelley's *Frankenstein.*" *Byron Journal* 19 (1991): 26–40.

Davis, James P. "*Frankenstein* and the Subversion of the Male Voice." *Women's Studies* 21 (1992): 307–22.

Dickerson, Vanessa D. "The Ghost of a Self: Female Identity in Mary Shelley's *Frankenstein.*" *Journal of Popular Culture* 27, No. 3 (Winter 1993): 79–91.

Dunn, Jane. *Moon in Eclipse: A Life of Mary Shelley.* New York: St. Martin's Press, 1978.

Dussinger, John A. "Kinship and Guilt in Mary Shelley's *Frankenstein.*" *Studies in the Novel* 8 (1976): 38–55.

Forry, Steven Earl. *Hideous Progenies: Dramatizations of* Frankenstein *from Mary Shelley to the Present.* Philadelphia: University of Pennsylvania Press, 1990.

Gilbert, Sandra. "Horror's Twin: Mary Shelley's Monstrous Eve." *Feminist Studies* 4, No. 2 (June 1978): 48–73.

Glut, Donald F. *The Frankenstein Catalog.* Jefferson, NC: McFarland, 1981.

———. *The Frankenstein Legend: A Tribute to Mary Shelley and Boris Karloff.* Metuchen, NJ: Scarecrow Press, 1973.

Harris Smith, Susan. "*Frankenstein:* Mary Shelley's Psychic Divisiveness." *Women and Literature* 5 (1977): 42–53.

Hill, J. M. "Frankenstein and the Physiognomy of Desire." *American Imago* 32 (1975): 332–58.

Hirsch, Gordon D. "The Monster Was a Lady: On the Psychology of Mary Shelley's *Frankenstein.*" *Hartford Studies in Literature* 7 (1975): 116–53.

Hobbs, Colleen. "Reading the Symptoms: An Exploration of Repression and Hysteria in Mary Shelley's *Frankenstein.*" *Studies in the Novel* 25 (1993): 152–69.

Hodges, Devon. "*Frankenstein* and the Feminine Subversion of the Novel." *Tulsa Studies in Women's Literature* 2 (1983): 155–64.

Jacobus, Mary. "Is There a Woman in This Text?" *New Literary History* 13 (1982): 117–41.

Kiely, Robert. *The Romantic Novel in England.* Cambridge, MA: Harvard University Press, 1972.

Kranzler, Laura. "*Frankenstein* and the Technological Future." *Foundation* No. 44 (Winter 1988–89): 42–49.

Levine, George, and U. C. Knoepflmacher, ed. *The Endurance of* Frankenstein. Berkeley: University of California Press, 1979.

London, Bette. "Mary Shelley, *Frankenstein,* and the Spectacle of Masculinity." *PMLA* 108 (1993): 253–67.

Lowe-Evans, Mary. Frankenstein: *Mary Shelley's Wedding Guest.* New York: Twayne, 1993.

McInerney, Peter. "Frankenstein and the Godlike Science of Letters." *Genre* 13 (1980): 455–75.

Mellor, Anne Kostelanetz. *Mary Shelley: Her Life, Her Fiction, Her Monsters.* New York: Methuen, 1988.

Newman, Beth. "Narratives of Seduction and the Seductions of Narrative: The Frame Structure of *Frankenstein.*" *ELH* 53 (1986): 141–63.

O'Rourke, James. " 'Nothing More Unnatural': Mary Shelley's Revision of Rousseau." *ELH* 56 (1989): 543–69.

Perkins, Margo V. "The Nature of Otherness: Class and Difference in Mary Shelley's *Frankenstein.*" *Studies in the Humanities* 19 (1992): 27–42.

Phy, Allene Stuart. *Mary Shelley.* Mercer Island, WA: Starmont House, 1988.

Poovey, Mary. "My Hideous Progeny: Mary Shelley and the Feminization of Romanticism." *PMLA* 95 (1980): 332–47.

Rubinstein, Marc A. " 'My Accursed Origin': The Search for the Mother in *Frankenstein.*" *Studies in Romanticism* 15 (1976): 165–94.

Seed, David. "*Frankenstein:* Parable or Spectacle?" *Criticism* 24 (1982): 327–40.

Sherwin, Paul. "*Frankenstein:* Creation as Catastrophe." *PMLA* 96 (1981): 883–903.

Small, Christopher. *Ariel Like a Harpy: Shelley, Mary and Frankenstein.* London: Gollancz, 1972.

Spark, Muriel. *Mary Shelley.* New York: Dutton, 1987.

Sunstein, Emily W. *Mary Shelley: Romance and Reality.* Boston: Little, Brown, 1989.

Tillotson, Marcia. "A Forced Solitude: Mary Shelley and the Creation of Frankenstein's Monster." In *The Female Gothic,* ed. Juliann E. Fleenor. Montreal: Eden Press, 1983, pp. 167–75.

Walling, William A. *Mary Shelley.* New York: Twayne, 1972.

Youngquist, Paul. "*Frankenstein:* The Mother, the Daughter, and the Monster." *Philological Quarterly* 70 (1991): 339–59.

Index of
Themes and Ideas